Good Work!

Get a *GREAT JOB* or be your *OWN BOSS*: a young person's guide

Nancy Schaefer

CERIC
Canadian Education and Research
Institute for Counselling

Good Work!

Published and distributed in 2005 by
The Canadian Education and Research Institute for Counselling
with the support of The Counselling Foundation of Canada

The Canadian Education and Research Institute for Counselling
18 Spadina Road, Suite 200
Toronto, Ontario, Canada M5R 2S7
Tel. (416) 929-2510
www.ceric.ca

05 04 03 02 01 1 2 3 4 5

Library and Archives Canada Cataloguing in Publication

Schaefer, Nancy (Nancy Elizabeth)
Good work! : get a great job or be your own boss :
a young person's guide
/ Nancy Schaefer

Previous ed. published Toronto : Stoddart, 2000 under title: Good job!
Includes Index.
ISBN 0-9687840-3-8

1. Job hunting. 2. Self-employed. 3. Youth–Employment. I. Canadian
Education and Research Institute for Counselling. II. Title.

HF5382.7.S323 2005   650.14'084'2   C2005-903406-8

Cartoon Illustrations: Anthony Stanberry Freeze DNA
www.freeze-dna.com

Cover Design: Jack Steiner

Printed and bound in Canada on 100% recycled post-consumer waste paper
(old-growth-forest free)

For all young people
who are looking for work
or starting their own business,
and the people who have the honour
of helping them

Contents

Chapter 8: All About Interviews   96

How is this book different?

Getting a job isn't always easy, especially if you're young. When I wrote *Good Job! A Young Person's Guide to Finding, Landing, and Loving a Job*, I included everything you needed to know about getting a job. This book has lots of updated information, such as tips for Internet job searching, yet continues to give you all the skills to land a job to love.

But if you've dreamed of starting your own business or have taken those first steps towards doing so, then this is the right book for you. Now, *Good Work!* includes specific information on how to start a business.

For over four decades our organization, Youth Employment Service (YES), has helped thousands of youth to find jobs and careers. Since the late nineties we have also helped hundreds of young people who want to start their own business. We opened Canada's first youth business centre in 1998. This book is based on our experience and success in helping younger people to launch businesses.

Like many young people, you may not want to work for someone else. You have a dream, a great idea, and the personal skills to work for yourself. This book will help you at every stage of developing your business.

This book is different because it's written expressly for younger people. It's written in plain, easy-to-understand language, gives straightforward advice, and speaks to your individual issues around finding a job or starting a business.

Life is an exciting journey. Work is part of that journey and provides money to live, along with challenge and fulfillment. Whether you work for someone else or manage you own business, remember to enjoy the trip. You can go wherever you want, accomplish any goal . . . but you need to believe in yourself. I wrote this book because I believe in your youth, your energy, and your skills; I know you can succeed.

Nancy Schaefer

Acknowledgements

I feel blessed to have such talented and dedicated people help me with this project.

I work with a wonderful team of talented staff at YES. The information, advice and lessons learned in this book came from all of them. Thank you to the staff at YES. In particular, I want to thank Margaret Douglas and Sinead McCarthy. They effectively manage the programs and services at YES and without their daily assistance and competency I would not have been able to write this book.

The YES team is too large to mention everyone's name. I thank them all. People like Shoshana Fainsilber, Amutha Vipulananda, Raymond Ju, Elaine Yang, Michael Raymond, and Charlotte Steeves have been with me for many years. They deserve so much credit for their work. They keep our organization at the forefront of youth issues.

I am also grateful to all of our supporters ... the many individuals, volunteers, foundations, and corporations. YES, with the generous support from the Ontario Ministry of Training, Colleges and Universities, Human Resources and Skills Development Canada, the City of Toronto and The Rotary Club of Toronto, has helped thousands upon thousands of youth find jobs or start a business. I thank them all.

I have also been fortunate to work for an outstanding volunteer Board of Directors. Because of their generous commitment to volunteering and to helping young people we have built together a great organization. Thank you to each one for your support and encouragement.

Thanks also to the fabulous young people who provided their experience and feedback. In focus groups and one-on-one interviews, they provided me with a wealth of valuable advice. They opened their hearts to share this information with our readers. That's why this book is special ... real people, young people sharing their experiences so that you can learn from their mistakes and successes.

This book further develops my earlier book ... *Good Job! A Young Person's Guide to Finding, Landing and Loving a Job.* Both books were written with the direct input of many young people. I thank all those who made the earlier book possible, including the Atkinson Foundation and Jonathan Bennett.

Thanks to the team at Colborne Communcations. Greg Iannou, Jennie Worden and Jack Steiner helped with every aspect of the book. They kept me focused and provided immense assistance.

Most important are my children, Victoria and Amanda van Schouwen. They are the love of my life. Amanda is still a teenager as I write this book so I know about all the fun and the troubles of being a teenager from her. Amanda and I have worked side by side on her job searches. She's a delight to live with. We have learned and succeeded together. Amanda knows about the excitement and challenges with my work, my volunteering in the community and my personal practices. I thank her for her patience and support. Victoria is a university student and works part time as a waitress in a vegan restaurant. She plans to be a teacher when she finishes school. Victoria has tried all kinds of different part time jobs; she's a great example of a young person who can do anything she puts her mind to. I love my children and thank them for being in my life.

The support of the Counselling Foundation of Canada has been outstanding. Huge thanks to the Board of Directors of the

Foundation for approving initial funding for this project and to Jean Faulds. The Counselling Foundation of Canada is one of the pioneers of career counselling in Canada. They understand that the key to prosperous communities and individual well-being is to nurture economic and individual diversity. Citizens of every age benefit from receiving career and employment counselling, and successful new businesses can provide additional jobs for young people and others.

Finally, this book has been the result of a partnership between YES and the Canadian Education and Research Institute for Counselling (CERIC). CERIC's efforts are directed at increasing the economic and social wealth and productivity of Canadians through improved quality, effectiveness and accessibility of career counselling and career development programs. I thank CERIC for publishing this book, and Riz Ibrahim and all those connected with CERIC.

I am grateful and honored to be able to bring this exciting new information to the public. I thank all of you.

Nancy Schaefer

Starting Out

"Hey! I need a job."

Each year, in every province, many thousands of young Canadians come to the very same conclusion: "Hey! I need a job."

If you're one of them, then you're probably feeling all sorts of things right now. Along with realizing that you have to — or want to — look for a job come many different emotions, like the excitement of new experiences and the thrill that you'll be earning your own money. But for some people who have not had much work experience, the idea of job searching can also be a little scary.

If you're feeling scared, or frustrated, or you don't know where to start — or if you're worried that no employer would hire someone like you — then you've come to the right place. Deciding that it's time to get a job means you want to take action. So let's get at it.

Will having a job mean I'm different now?

There's no doubt about it: working will affect your life in many new ways. Working is not like school. At work, people expect different things from you; you'll also discover different rewards, feel different pressures, and experience different successes and achievements.

What can a job do for me?

Having a job, whether it's a part-time job during the school year, a summer job, or a full-time job after you're done with school, is a great way to gain the respect, freedom, and independence you deserve.

Having a job will give you money to buy the things you need and want. It will help you pay for your life. You will be able to help others around you, like your parents, girlfriend or boyfriend, siblings, or roommates, because you'll be taking better care of your own needs.

Here's what some young Canadians have said about their first year at work:

"I like it. I work in a restaurant three nights a week. It's hard sometimes, long hours. But the tips are pretty good. I'm saving for a car."

— Brendan, age 18, Fredericton, NB

"I worked in a store last summer. My uncle got me the job. I have to make money for university."

— Eva, age 16, Montreal, QC

"I'm working as a labourer. I work for one guy who owns a small landscape company. It's just me and him. In the summer we do yard work. Winter we plough snow and do other odd jobs. We get along pretty good. When I dropped out of school, he just hired me. He took a chance on me."

— Joe, age 17, Hamilton, ON

"I help out my mom and dad on the farm. I've always done it. But now that I'm older it's changed things a little. I have to do it, not just when I feel like it."

— Jenny, age 15, North Battleford, SK

"My older brother started a business designing web pages and I help him. He works full-time and I work part-time, full-time in the summer. It's been going for almost a year now. I like working from home but he pays me only when he can — it's hard starting your own business at the beginning. But I'm just doing it for the experience because I want to be a computer programmer."

— Sanjay, age 16, Richmond, BC

So as you can see, there are many, many different types of jobs. Some young people work part-time during the school year, others work only in the summers, while some have finished with school and are working full-time.

What jobs can I do?

The secret is to discover what you are already good at, what you already enjoy doing, and start looking there.

Warning: As someone just starting out in the workforce, you'll find that it's hard to get that "dream job." Sure, we all know that lucky someone who seems to have the best job going, but job searching is all about planning and being realistic.

Yes, it's a better idea to take a job that you want rather than just any job. But it's not always that easy. For some, the money — getting a paycheque — is the most important thing, and the sooner it arrives, the better. If that's you, then take the first job you can; but remember, your future is open and you don't have to accept "just any job" for long. For now, work and earn that money you need. But keep looking. Your dream job *will* come one day, and the most important step to getting it is to start somewhere. That's where you are right now.

Your first few jobs will give you important experience to move toward your dream job or help you build a fulfilling career. Even if you don't know yet what the dream job is, every job requires experience. Now is the best time to begin to build it. So let's get started.

It's important to know your skills and interests. Even if you've never had a job before, you still have many interests and skills that employers will look for.

A QUICK THREE-STEP GUIDE TO FOCUS YOUR JOB SEARCH

Ask yourself:

1. What kinds of jobs do I find interesting?
2. Why do these jobs interest me?
3. What am I already good at?

Here are some other questions to help you decide what kinds of jobs you might like to do:

- Do I like working with people?
- Do I like working with my hands?
- Do I like working with computers and technology?
- Do I like working in a team?
- Do I prefer working on my own?
- Do I like working during the days or at night?
- Do I mind working on the weekends?
- Do I like working outside?
- Do I like talking to people on the phone?
- Do I like convincing people and selling ideas?
- Do I like to read a lot?

What kinds of jobs do other youth get?

Here is a list of typical jobs for young people in Canada. Of course, the jobs vary from province to province and from season to season, but this is a good starting point:

- Retail jobs in shops, mall stores, department stores, grocery stores, movie cinemas, superstores, gas stations, video stores.
- Service jobs, such as waiter/waitress, table busser, cook, host/hostess, bell hop, front desk attendant, server, cashier, kitchen support worker.
- General labouring jobs, which might involve painting, window cleaning, cutting lawns, snow removal, leaf removal, house cleaning, landscaping, labour at building sites, warehouses, and factories.
- All kinds of short-term jobs found through temp agencies.
- Summer jobs, such as lifeguard, parks and rec. worker, landscaper, camp counsellor, tree planter, tour guide, house painter, amusement park worker, child care worker.
- Office jobs, such as filing clerk, telemarketer, web designer, secretary, receptionist, data entry clerk, administrative assistant, word processor.
- Government jobs. Many government departments hire young people for both summer and permanent work. Check out the government websites, or ask a guidance counsellor or employment counsellor.

TEMP AGENCIES are companies that find short-term work assignments for skilled workers by matching them with employers who need help for just a few days or weeks. If you are interested in joining a temp agency, look in the Yellow Pages under "employment."

Deciding on what kind of job you would like to do can be tough, but the choice is yours to make. Take control of your job search. It's not just a matter of filling out applications and waiting by the phone for employers to call you back. You can take steps to make sure you get those calls!

When you narrow down what kind of job you would like, it's time to do a little research. Ask around, check out the Internet, and find out more about the areas you are interested in. How do other people get jobs in those fields? It's up to you to discover the many ways to get what you want.

RESEARCHING a job means to gather information about a position. This includes finding out about duties, responsibilities, pay, location, and hours of work.

Why do young people get jobs?

Young people get different types of jobs for different reasons. Here are some:

- to make money
- to get experience
- to get respect
- to save for a car
- for something to do
- to have freedom
- to be independent
- to save for school
- because friends have jobs
- to pay rent and bills

- to save for a trip
- to learn about a potential career

I don't have any idea what kind of job I want!

Don't worry if you can't decide on the kind of job you want to look for. It happens to everyone. In fact, most people question the kind of job they want many, many times in their life.

Because working is still pretty new to you, and you haven't experienced work life for long, it's hard to decide what you might like to do. If this is you, then here are some options:

- Get some job advice from an employment agency. (Check out Chapter 17 of this book for help in finding a centre near you.)
- Do a general job search and see what you can find. Who knows, once you get started, something you see advertised might appeal to you.
- If you have a few different possibilities but can't narrow it down, ask someone you know if you can spend some time "job shadowing" them. Job shadowing means you spend an hour or two with someone on the job to see first-hand what is involved in that position. Perhaps a friend is doing a job that you might like. Ask them to ask their boss if you can hang out for a while and help so you can see if the job appeals to you.

What is a part-time job?

Some students who live at home with their family get part-time jobs during the school year to gain work experience. Other students are saving for things they want, like a car, or a holiday, or money to go to college or university. Still other youth in school work just to earn some spending money. Many students take jobs for a combination of all these reasons. Working part-time after school or on the weekends just makes good sense.

What is a summer job?

Almost all students fill their summer holidays with work of some variety, even if it's volunteer work. Having a summer job is a great chance to gain experience in the workforce, make new friends outside school, and, in most cases, earn money. Some students focus on getting jobs that will help them learn about careers they might like to pursue later on, while others are simply interested in making as much money as they can while school's out.

What is a full-time job?

Whether it's before or after graduation, at some point everyone finishes with school. The next step is either to get more education or to get a full-time job. If you feel like school is not where you want to be at the moment, then full-time jobs are necessary because they give you the money to support yourself, pay rent, buy food and CDs or DVDs, and even to save a little. When you're not in school, working full-time makes you feel good. It gives you a steady income, lets you plan ahead, and gives you the power to take control of your life. It's hard to get by if you're not in school and don't have a full-time job. Some people even get more than one part-time job to give them full-time hours.

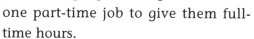

A full-time job can give you the opportunity to plan and save. It's a great way to get what you want.

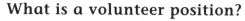

What is a volunteer position?

A volunteer job is an unpaid position. It gives you on-the-job experience that will help you get a paying job later. It can also help someone in need, or benefit animals or the environment. Volunteering is very important because it shows that you care about your local community, and it gives you skills and experience. If you are not going to get paid work right now, or if you feel you have some extra time, then the best thing you can do is to volunteer. It makes you and those around you feel good, and employers love to see it on a résumé.

What if I'd rather work than be in school?

Everyone tells you to stay in school, right? But are they really right? Is it right for *you*?

If you've dropped out of school, you'll know this is true: getting a full-time job without a high school diploma is not easy. It's not impossible — people do it every day — but don't be fooled, it is hard.

It's hard because so many people in Canada have a high school diploma and that makes the competition for jobs very tough for those without one. It's even a minimum requirement for many entry-level jobs.

ENTRY-LEVEL JOBS are positions that require the least amount of previous work experience or education.

Also, the kinds of jobs you can get with a high school diploma are often much higher paying and are probably better jobs than those you can get without one. It's just a fact of life.

Whether it's right or wrong, many employers believe that staying in school shows that you can finish something, that you can complete something you started.

So if you can, stay in school. But if you can't, plan ahead. Talk to your parents, or older brothers or sisters, or a guidance counsellor about your future after school. Ask them to help you think about what you want to do after high school is over for you. Start thinking about it now. You can't even begin to imagine all the many different courses offered at community colleges. Look at some material in the guidance office. Surf the web and look up colleges in your area. Find out what it takes to get there. Yes, getting an education is expensive, but it'll pay off in the end. Dream a little . . . it'll come true if you want it badly enough.

If you can't stay in school, if you simply must have a job and money to support yourself now, then don't despair. Read this book and collect your thoughts. There is a job out there for you and it will help you get the things you need like money for rent and food and clothes. Start looking for a job today. Once you know how and where to look, you won't believe how many employers need someone like you.

The good news is that there are many youth employment centres right across Canada that will help you find a full-time job. (Check out Chapter 17 of this book for help in finding a centre near you.) They have people there who are experts in helping young Canadians like you find full-time work . . .

- even if you didn't finish up to grade 12
- even if you're not sure where you want to work
- even if you're supporting a child
- even if you don't have a résumé
- even if you've never really had a job before
- even if you've left home
- even if you're new to Canada
- even if you have a criminal record.

The staff at youth employment centres will help you take many of the steps outlined in this book, so give the centre nearest you a call. Searching for a job can be hard if you're new at it. You don't have to do it alone.

2

Preparing for a Job Search

"Where do I start?"

There are a few basic things you'll need to have ready before you can begin to look for a job. Take the time to get them in place before you start and avoid hassles later on.

CHECKLIST — THE BASICS

- a Social Insurance Number (SIN)
- a phone number with an answering machine or voice mail
- references
- time set aside for job searching
- a positive attitude
- a nice set of clothes for interviews
- access to help for your job search, if needed

Do I need a Social Insurance Number, or SIN?

Everyone should have a Social Insurance Number (it's called a SIN for short). It's a form of identification necessary for getting a job. A SIN is a nine-digit number, given to you on a plastic card. When the Government of Canada gives you your number, it allows you to work because you'll need to give it to your employer when you get hired. The SIN is used for your taxes, employment insurance, and pensions. You might also need it for other things like applying to get into college, university, or other types of further education.

How do I get a SIN?

There are several ways you can get an application form for a SIN. The best is to go to your local Human Resources Centre of Canada (HRCC) office and pick up an application. You can find the one nearest to you by looking up "Social Insurance Numbers" in the Government of Canada section of your local phone book. It's the "blue pages" section. Also, you can call and ask to have an application form mailed to you, or you can download it from the website of Human Resources Development Canada (HRDC), which is the ministry that oversees all the HRCC offices in Canada. You could also ask a friend who already works where they got their application form.

After you've filled in the form, follow the instructions carefully. You will see that when you return to the office to hand in the form, you will need to bring documentation proving your identity and status in Canada. It is also possible to mail in your application and supporting documents. There is no fee to apply for an initial SIN number.

For more information call your local HRCC office or visit HRDC online at the following website: www.hrdc-drhc.gc.ca.

Remember, a SIN is a private number. You are not legally required to give it to an employer until you are hired.

What if I never get my telephone messages around here?

A reliable telephone number, with voice mail, is extremely important while you are job searching. It is important for an employer to be able to reach you at any time and leave a message if you are not home. Make sure the "greeting" you have on the machine is basic and professional. While you're job searching it's best to avoid humorous messages.

If you share the telephone with other people, tell them you are job searching. Make sure they know how important it is that you get your messages promptly, and that they will need to take down all the details.

If you do not have a telephone number, there are many youth employment services (see Chapter 17) that can set you up with a voice-mail number. Also, you could ask a friend to let you use their number while you are looking for a job.

What are references?
A reference is someone who agrees to speak to a potential employer about you and your abilities in a positive way.

What is a reference letter?
A reference letter is a professional letter written by a previous employer, teacher, coach, or someone else who can honestly speak about your skills and abilities. Most employers will want to speak directly to your reference; however, some might also accept a reference letter.

TIP Always make photocopies of a reference letter to give to employers. At an interview, have the original with you in case the employer asks to see it, but let them keep only a photocopy.

It's always a good idea to ask your supervisor for a reference letter when you leave a job or volunteer position. This is especially true if you know it will be difficult for an employer to contact your reference in the future.

Who should I choose to be my references?
The best reference is your last employer. They know better than anyone how you performed on the job. This is why, where possible, it is important to leave a job on good terms and ask for a reference letter.

How can I get references if I'm looking for my first job?

Most employers who are hiring for entry-level positions understand that young people don't have much or any work experience and therefore won't have previous employers as references. If this is your first job search, a reference can also be a teacher, a coach, clergy, or someone you volunteered for. The important thing is to ask someone who knows you and thinks highly of you.

Who cannot be one of my references?

A reference cannot be someone who is related to you. This includes your parents, uncles, aunts, cousins, siblings, step-parents, and grandparents. Girlfriends or boyfriends are also not appropriate references. Even using a friend is not recommended. An employer will only be impressed by positive comments about you if they come from someone who does not feel obliged. Whatever you do, never use someone who shares your address and phone number.

When you give your references to an employer, you have to say what your relationship is to that person, and when that relationship occurred. Don't lie.

If you can't use a previous employer, or you don't have one, it's best to pick someone older than you, and someone who has supervised you in some way, like a teacher, youth worker, or coach.

What will a reference need to say about me?

A reference will have to be able to tell an employer that you are (for example) . . .

- a good person
- a hard worker
- reliable
- honest
- punctual
- trustworthy
- a fast learner.

A reference is not a character witness. They have to be able to give concrete examples of your skills and abilities. Choose someone who has supervised you in some way. It's best if they have known you for a number of years.

Is it a big deal to ask someone to be a reference?

Yes, and you will find people will want to be honest. So choose someone you like and who likes you. Most importantly, ask their permission. Here's how you might want to approach a potential reference:

- "Hi, Ms. _____ , it's _____ _____ . I'm about to start looking for a job as a _____ . I was wondering if you would mind being a reference for me?"

Tell your references you will call them and let them know when you have an interview. Keep them informed of your job search.

TIP Not only is it polite to warn a reference when they can expect a call — it's to your advantage. A reference who knows about the specific job you're applying for is more prepared and is more likely to answer an employer's questions with examples that are well thought out.

When do I have to give my references?

Some employers insist on references being listed right when you first apply on an application form, while others won't ask for them until an interview. Not all employers check references, but most do. That's why it's best to be prepared with your references before you start your job search.

How long will my job search take?

It's difficult to say because everybody is different: a few days, a week, perhaps months. It will take time, but if you stick with it and follow the advice in this book it will shorten the time it takes. You'll get that job.

It's a good idea to keep a list of all the places you contact in your job search. Keep track of the names of the companies and the people you talk to when you visit or call, because employers may keep your résumé "on file." This means that if you don't get the job this time, they will keep you in mind for a future position. It's not uncommon to receive a call from an employer weeks, even months, after you dropped off your résumé. So keep note of the places where you've applied. If a potential employer calls you back, you'll want to remember where they are located and who you talked to there.

What if I'm too busy right now to look for a job?

It takes a lot of time to get a job. As you'll often hear people say, "it's a full-time job getting a job." Make sure you have the time. Sure, sometimes we get lucky and find success on the first day. But, sadly, this is not usually the case. Putting in an hour or two a week won't be enough.

Also, when you start getting interviews, it takes time to get to where the interview is held, and time to get home. Make sure you leave yourself enough time on the days you have interviews. You don't want to be rushed or show up late.

Most importantly, make sure you are ready to start, and that you have time to work. Having a job is an important commitment. When you are scheduled to work, you have to be there. You can't just miss a day for no good reason. Make sure that if you accept a job, working will not get in the way of any other important commitments you may have, like school. You can't be in two places at once.

TIP Job searching needs a positive attitude. You will get a job. You must stay at it and try your best. It will happen. Look around you at all the people who go to work every day. At one time, they were in the same position as you are. They made it, and you will too. If you can prepare for some rejection, it'll be easier to continue on until you hear those words: "I'd like to offer you the job." If you think you are good enough for the job, an employer will, too.

How much will my job search cost me?

Job searching costs some money. Although there are employment centres you can go to for free help and services, such as free Internet access, free faxing, and free newspapers, job searching can still cost money. If you take the bus, it costs money to get to an interview. To buy a nice set of clothes for interviews will also cost money. If you are having financial difficulties with your job search, be sure to contact the nearest youth employment service provider near you. They can often arrange for free transportation to interviews and provide you with access to clothes for interviews.

What if I don't have an address or phone number right now?

If you are living temporarily away from home, on the street, or in a shelter, you still have options. There are many free services that can help you search for a job. They can often help you get connected to housing services and social assistance in your community, and get you a free phone number and voice mailbox to use while you are looking for work. There are always options; in most cases, all you need to do is ask. Read Chapter 17 of this book for help in finding an employment service near you. There are experts ready to help you find a job if you can't manage it on your own. Everyone knows that finding a job is hard when you're young. The important thing is to ask for help.

What if I really need money today?

Job searching takes time. It's a simple fact that for most young people, job searching means facing some rejection. That's why it's important to keep at it and to not give up. It's common for youth looking for first jobs to only get one interview for every twenty résumés they submit. And that's just getting an interview. Actually getting a job may take several interviews. This might seem discouraging, but look at it another way — getting good at interviews takes practice and now your skills have improved.

If you need a full-time job today because you are desperate for money to pay rent or buy food, call a nearby employment centre today. They can get you connected to government programs that will help you if you're in urgent need.

TIPS

- Get started as early as you can. Take the first step as soon as possible.
- Have a positive attitude. You will get that job.
- Following the advice in this book will help you get a job sooner.
- Rejection does not mean you won't get a job, or that you are not a capable person. Rejection happens to everyone, and it's a normal part of job searching.
- Have a reliable phone line with voice mail, and remind your friends or family to take detailed messages while you are job searching.

3

The Application Form

"Don't I just have to fill it out and give it to them?"

Think of the application form as the first step to getting an interview. Take it home and fill it in carefully. Then, return the application, paper-clipped together with your résumé and cover letter, to the employer. Including a résumé and cover letter (see Chapters 4 and 5) is an extra step but it may put you ahead of the other applicants. It shows your interest in the position is serious.

What is an application form?

An application form is a sheet, often double-sided, that is used by employers to check out potential candidates for a job. Application forms are tools to help employers obtain some basic information from you and ask you some simple questions about yourself, your employment history, education level, and other qualifications.

Will every job that I want to apply for have an application form?

No, but many entry-level, part-time, and summer positions do, so it is important to know how to fill them in correctly.

Employers that typically use application forms include summer camps, government, retail stores, restaurants and fast food outlets, warehouses, factories, temp agencies, pools, amusement parks, video stores, cinemas, and telemarketing companies.

The good news is that application forms are easy to obtain, and they treat each potential candidate equally.

How do I get an application form?

Most places that use application forms require you to apply in person. Stores, restaurants, and government offices will all have application forms available for you to pick up. It's a good idea to call the employer before you go in and ask if they have application forms to fill in.

What should I say when I get there?
What if I'm too embarrassed?

It sometimes feels difficult to just go up to someone who is working and ask for an application form. But lots of people do it every day. Once you've asked for one application form, you'll see it's no big deal and it just takes a second.

Who should I speak to?

Most employees can give you an application form but the best plan is to ask to speak to the manager. So keep in mind that even when you're just picking up the form there is a good chance that you will meet the person who does the hiring. Dress nicely, smile, and be sure to introduce yourself to whoever gives you the form. You want to make a strong first impression. If they remember you, it might be what gets you an interview later.

TIP Find out the name of the hiring manager. Write it down and get the correct spelling. You're going to need it when you're writing your cover letter. If you forget to ask while you're picking up the application form, call them back later to find out. You might say something like:

"Hi. My name is _____ _____ and I picked up an application form earlier today. I'm just about to do a cover letter and I wonder if you could tell me the name of the hiring manager?"

TIP Collect the application form from the employer and take it home. Don't fill it in nearby and drop it off twenty minutes later. Filling in an application form takes time to do well and it must be done neatly. Also, that way you will be able to customize your résumé and cover letter for each different application you make. Standard résumés and cover letters are impersonal and are not as successful as those that have been written specifically for each application.

What will I need to know when I'm filling one out?

Correct contact information
This means your name, address, and phone number.
Other information
Application forms frequently ask you to name the schools you've attended and describe any previous positions you've held. Be sure to include volunteer positions. *Warning:* You will need to know when you started and finished working your previous jobs.

Hours of availability
Try to be as available as you possibly can.
Names and phone numbers of references
Although it is not recommended to give out names of references on your résumé or cover letter, application forms sometimes ask for them. If this is the case you can write "available on request" in that space and, if you get an interview, bring along a sheet listing your references, or copies of your reference letters if you have any. If you choose to include them on the application form, remember to ask permission from your references first. Tell them that you are job searching and filling out applications and that they may receive a call.

But doesn't my résumé say all this again?

Yes, there will be some overlap between your résumé and the application form, but you must go to the extra trouble. Filling in an application form does not replace the need for a résumé or cover letter. You should still hand in all three. They are all equally important and doing this will really increase your chances of getting an interview.

LOOK AT IT FROM THE EMPLOYER'S POINT OF VIEW

If an employer at a store in a mall receives fifty-four application forms, one of the ways he or she will separate them into "yes" and "no" piles is by looking at how completely, neatly, and accurately the applications are filled in. An employer definitely wants an employee who can follow the simple instructions on the form and looks organized.

Ten Steps to Completing a Successful Application Form

1. Be prepared and look professional.

When you go out to pick up application forms, look your best. Bring along a notebook or pad of paper, plus a pen. You should keep track of every employer you visit and every employee you talk with. It'll help you remember if you don't hear back for a few weeks.

2. Smile and be polite.

When you go into the place where you want to apply, ask if you can speak to a manager. Be very polite and speak clearly. If the manager doesn't want to be disturbed, then just direct your questions to the person you are already speaking with.

3. Ask for two application forms.

Again, be very polite and ask if you can have two application forms. You can say something like: "I'm interested in applying for a job here. Is there an application form?" If there is an application, then say: "I'd like two copies if possible please." If you can't get two, then photocopy the form before you begin to fill it out. That way you'll have one to practise on first.

4. Get as much information as possible.

Finding out more about the workplace will help you decide if this is the right job for you. If the person you're talking to seems friendly and isn't too busy, ask them about the position. You could ask if they know when they will be scheduling interviews, or how many hours they expect people to work. If they are busy, it is best to keep it short. Just make sure to get the name of the manager in charge of hiring.

5. Take the application home and fill it out.

Do a thorough, very neat job. Make sure to get help from a friend or parent when filling out parts that you aren't sure about.

6. Attach a résumé and cover letter (see Chapters 4 and 5 for more help).

Even if the employer doesn't ask for a résumé and cover letter, do them anyway. It will make you look more organized. Try to include in your cover letter any information you collected when you picked up the application.

7. Return the application directly to the person doing the hiring.

Before you return your application, call first. If you weren't able to find out the person's name when you picked up your application, this is also a good time to find it out. Handing your application directly to the person doing the hiring will improve your chances of being chosen for an interview.

8. Remember the name of the person who took your application.

If the person in charge of hiring is not available, don't worry. Write down the name of the person who takes your application. Call back later or the next day to speak to the person doing the hiring and say, "I brought in my application yesterday and gave it to _____ _____ . I just wanted to make sure you received it."

9. Don't try too hard, or annoy the manager.

If you're calling just to see whether or not they got your résumé, try not to ask for any other information. Hopefully you already know when they're doing the hiring. If not, that should be the only other thing you ask at this point. Don't ask for details about the job. You don't want to bother them and hurt your chances.

10. Call back to check on your application a few days before they said they'd be interviewing.

It's okay to call the person you know is in charge of hiring just to say, "I just wanted to check on my application." It will be clear that you are interested and that you're organized enough to have kept track. This will give a great impression at the critical time when they are deciding who to interview.

Warning: If you are told "Don't call us, we'll call you if you are chosen for an interview," or something similar, don't call. Always follow the employer's instructions.

What questions should I ask when I'm handing in the application form?

Here are some good things to ask and say when you're handing in your application. When you first drop it off, you might say:

- "Hi. I'm _____ _____ . I'm dropping off my application for the _____ position that is available. Can I please speak to the person doing the hiring?"

If you manage to get introduced to the person doing the hiring, try asking some questions:

- "Can you tell me a little bit more about the position?"
- "Do you have any idea of when you will be scheduling interviews?"

If you have an opportunity, tell them you are interested in the position:

- "As you'll be able to see from my application, I'm really interested in the position. This looks like a great place to work."

Always remember to dress nicely, smile, shake the manager's hand firmly, and confidently thank them:

- "I appreciate your taking a few moments to speak with me. I hope to hear from you soon."

What if they ask a question that I think is private or personal?

In Canada, there are laws that govern the relationship between you and your employer, and they take effect and begin to protect you even before you are hired, when you are applying for jobs. Although the laws differ from province to province, you always are guaranteed certain rights.

If you think an employer has asked you an unfair question on an application, call or visit the website of your province's ministry of labour and find out. You can find the phone number in the "blue pages" of your phone book or by doing a search on the Internet. Know your rights.

Some applications just ask weird questions. If you come across a question that you think is irrelevant or strange, all you can do is try your best to answer it.

DOs AND DON'Ts OF APPLICATION FORMS

DOs

✓ Do take the form home and fill it in neatly, in blue or black pen, with no spelling errors.
✓ Do have someone you trust look it over for you.
✓ Do attach a cover letter and résumé.
✓ Do try to speak to the person doing the hiring whenever you can.
✓ Do dress well when you are handing in your application form.
✓ Do keep track of the places where you've applied.

DON'Ts

✗ Don't ever lie on an application form.
✗ Don't leave any parts blank, or questions unanswered.
✗ Don't write, "See attached on résumé." Always fill it out in full.

I need more help with my application form . . .

If you need more help with your application form, your nearest youth employment centre can help you. Check out Chapter 17 of this book for help in finding a centre near you. Also, remember that you can ask a friend, parent, or teacher to give you a hand. It's always a good idea to ask for some help when filling out application forms.

4

Résumés

"Do I really need one?"

Yes. Résumés are an important part of any job search because most employers insist on them as part of the application process. Whether you are looking for a part-time, summer, or full-time job, a well-written résumé will help you achieve success. Some young people worry that writing a résumé will be hard because they lack experience. That's understandable, but everyone needs a résumé, and they're not hard to write once you know how. Tell yourself that you can do it and that there is a job out there for you. Once you've written one résumé, it gets much easier.

What is a résumé?

A résumé is a short summary of who you are, what you have done, and what you can do. This includes your skills, abilities, work history, volunteer experience, education level, interests, and strengths. A résumé also states your full name, address, phone number, and, if you happen to have them, your fax number and e-mail address.

The good news is that your résumé should not be longer than one or two pages. If you have never had a job, or your work experience is limited, then one page is all that you need.

How should I start writing my résumé?

A great way to start thinking about the kind of job you might like to apply for is to simply start doing your résumé. Sitting down and writing your résumé will help you see exactly what it is you have to offer. Take a look at some sample résumés on pages 41–44 to get an idea of what a finished one looks like.

Now, start by making a list of all the different experiences you have had in school, after school, during the summers, and on weekends. Include all previous jobs, sports, volunteering, hobbies, clubs, and anything else you can think of. Next, make a second list of the skills and attributes that your experiences show. For example, you may be hard working, a team player, dedicated, a strong communicator, able to do many tasks at once, responsible. Once you've built a list, you're ready to begin!

I wrote a résumé last summer. Can I just use it again?

Because you change over time, so must your résumé. As you accomplish new things, your résumé should grow and change. Never just send off an old résumé. Always add in the new skills and experiences you've gained since the last time you wrote it. You will change your résumé over the course of your lifetime many, many times. Start now. In fact, with each new job you apply for, you should take a good look at your résumé and customize it.

TIP When updating your résumé, remember to customize your cover letter too.

How do I make my résumé reflect what an employer is looking for?

Ask yourself the following questions:

- Are the contents of my résumé in the best order?
- Are the most applicable experiences and skills listed first?
- Have I left out anything that would help me get the job? This includes volunteer experience, hobbies, and interests.

What should my résumé look like?

There is no "right" way to set up a résumé. A résumé should reflect who you are and what you do. How it looks is totally up to you but it must always be clean and neatly organized and it must honestly reflect your experience and skills. Also keep in mind that employers expect to find certain things on your résumé, and they expect them to be presented within some basic guidelines. But you do have a choice.

There are three basic types of résumés to choose from. The first two types are very standard résumés, and the third is a newer type — a combination of the other two types — that many young people choose. Take some time to decide which one of the three will best highlight what you can offer an employer.

Chronological résumés

A chronological résumé is the traditional type of résumé that lists your experiences by date. It is divided into sections such as work experience, education, volunteer experience, achievements and awards, and hobbies and interests. Your work experience should be listed in order, with the most recent position appearing first.

If you are looking for your first job, or you have not had a lot of work experience, this is probably not the best type of résumé for you. This style of résumé suits older workers who have been in the workforce for some years. It gives a history of their work experience. It is especially good for showing strong commitment to a company or organization. This is the type of résumé you will likely want to work toward in a few years.

Functional résumés

Because functional résumés emphasize skills and downplay lack of experience, they are great for young people who are looking for their first job, or who have not had many jobs. This type of résumé focuses on skills gained in volunteer work, hobbies, and sporting or extra-curricular activities.

Combination résumés

If you've had some work experience, but not a lot, you might want to choose to do a combination résumé. This is an approach that combines the best from both types of résumé styles mentioned above.

There is no doubt about it — employers like to see work experience, so if you only have a little (one or two previous jobs) then the combination résumé might be for you. On it you can list, as in a chronological résumé, your previous work experience, but you can also, as in a functional résumé, show the skills that you gained in other activities. For many young job searchers with a little work experience, this option is the most successful.

What goes into a résumé?
Name and address

No matter which style you choose, at the top of your résumé you should place your full name, address, and phone number in bold and slightly larger type than you use for the rest of the résumé. If you have a fax number or e-mail address, you should list these as well.

TIP Remember to have voice mail, with a short, polite message, on your phone line while you are job searching. Inform your family, or the people you live with, that you are job searching. Tell them it is important that you receive detailed messages. If you have an e-mail address and you decide to list it, make sure it is straightforward (like john_smith@internet.com or jsmith123@hotnet.ca — no slang or silly nicknames) and check it often. Listing your e-mail address is a good idea because it tells an employer that you are computer literate.

Career or job objective statement

It is a good idea to include a statement of your career or job objective at the beginning of your résumé only if you are:

- applying for the same position at many different places. For example, if you want to work as a waiter or waitress and you are applying to many different restaurants, or you want to work as a salesperson at a store and are applying to many different stores
  or
- planning to drop off your résumé to many different places.

In these cases, having a clear, straightforward objective is helpful because it tells an employer, at a glance, what kind of job you are interested in. This is especially true if there is no application form to fill out, or you do not intend to do a cover letter. (See Chapters 3 and 5 for information on application forms and cover letters.)

Most employers receive many résumés, which they put in a pile until it comes time to hire. That's when an objective statement helps an employer choose which candidates to interview.

SAMPLE OBJECTIVE STATEMENTS

- To obtain a full-time summer position working in retail
- To obtain a part-time position working as a prep cook
- To obtain a full-time position working in customer service

Remember, if you decide to change the kind of position you are applying for, you must change your objective statement. Don't make the mistake of faxing a résumé with the objective statement "To work as a waiter" to a company that is hiring a receptionist.

TIP Objective statements are not as effective as a cover letter that is written specifically for the job to which you are applying. Employers respond much better to the extra effort you demonstrate when you write a cover letter. Also, for tips on how best to approach employers, look at the chapter on application forms.

"Highlights of qualifications" or "summary of skills"

In a big pile of résumés, this section is a great way to quickly tell a busy employer about your strongest skills and qualifications. Your summary of skills should appear at the top of the page, just below your name and address, and it is usually written as a list.

Your experience

You're probably thinking, "It's hard to write a résumé when I don't have much work experience." That's true, but here's a way around it: consider a functional résumé. Check out the example on page 43. It is most important,

as a new job searcher, to de-emphasize your lack of work experience and incomplete education and to emphasize the skills you've gained in other areas of your life at school, at home, or in your community. What you don't have in work experience you do have in personal qualities, and this will convince an employer that you possess the qualities they are looking for, such as creativity, "being able to learn new things easily," and trustworthiness.

Work experience (no job too small)
If you've had a job or two, be sure to list them, even if they were only short-term. Even a part-time job for a few days or weeks is good work experience. You will need to show the name of the company, organization, or person you worked for; your position or title; the dates you worked; the company's location (city or town); and a description of the duties and skills you gained on the job. Check out the examples on pages 41–44.

TIP If you worked for only a short time, simply list the month, or the season, that you worked.

Volunteer experience
Volunteer experience is very important to anyone looking for a job, but it is especially important for you if you don't have a lot of work experience. It's never too late to start volunteering. A volunteer job gives an employer an indication of your interests and what you care about. Volunteer experience can be listed in a separate section or along with any work experience. Be sure to list the following:

- the name of the person, charity, or non-profit or community organization you volunteered for
- your position or title
- the dates you volunteered
- the general location

- a description of your duties
- a list of the skills you gained

Volunteering is excellent work experience to showcase on your résumé. It shows that you are someone who cares about your community and that you are willing to spend your own time to help others.

The skills that can be learned in volunteer jobs are also highly valued because they often require attractive qualities like . . .

- dedication
- caring
- understanding of other people's needs and wants
- an awareness of a larger community.

If you have never volunteered, you don't know what you're missing. Get involved with a cause or charity that is important to you. You'll feel good about yourself, help someone who is in need, and one day it might even help you get a job.

TIP If you're listing volunteer experience in the same section as paid work experience, call the whole section "relevant work experience" so you are not misleading the employer.

Education

It is important to list the schools you have attended and which grades you've completed or your expected year of graduation. If you have graduated, then be sure to list the diploma earned. It's a good idea to list specific courses that you enjoyed or did well in. It shows an employer your interests and strengths. If it's applicable to the position that you are applying for, be sure to list any relevant courses. For example, if you are looking for a job where you will be working with cash, and you have completed a math course, then be sure to list it.

Awards and achievements

If you have any awards or achievements, be sure to list them, even if they are not directly relevant to the position. They show an employer that you have been successful and recognized by others. Awards and achievements can be from many different areas of life and they show that you are well rounded. They could include any of the following:

- sports championships, team awards, other awards
- academic scholarships, awards, high grades, honour roll
- life-saving levels, CPR certification, swimming levels
- any licences that you may have obtained — driving, flying, boating
- any language that you speak fluently

Hobbies and interests

Almost everyone has hobbies or interests. They are a great way to show an employer that you are good at different things. Who knows, an employer may share your love of computers, or dance, or chess, or hockey. Hobbies and interests show you as someone who is outgoing, interested in learning, dedicated, and focused. Try not to repeat your awards and achievements in this section.

TIP Don't list any hobbies or interests that won't help you get a job. "I am an avid reader" or "I enjoy many sports" or "I love to cook" are good, but "I like to watch TV" or "I love shopping" or "I love to go clubbing" or "I like to hang with friends" should be avoided.

What style of résumé should I pick?

It's up to you, but here are some guidelines:

- Your résumé should be on either standard plain white, off-white, or very light grey 8 ½" × 11" paper.

- Always type your résumé. If you don't have a computer, ask a friend if you can use theirs or go to your local employment resource centre (for help in finding one, read Chapter 17 of this book). NEVER write your résumé by hand.
- Use the same font style and size as your cover letter. Keep it simple.
- Single-space your résumé, keeping a double space between sections.
- Bold your name at the top, and repeat your name in the header of the second page, if you have a second page.
- Be sure to spellcheck your résumé, and have someone you trust read it over to make sure you don't have any spelling or grammatical errors.
- If you are applying to a specific industry, ask someone you know who already works in that industry to look over your résumé.

How should I send my résumé?

If you are responding to an advertisement that gives instructions on how the employer wishes to receive your application, then always follow the instructions. Respect an employer's wish for no phone calls if that is their request.

If they leave it up to you, or you are responding to a "help wanted" sign or a lead from a friend, or you are taking initiative and simply forwarding your résumé, then follow the basic guidelines on pages 54–55, in the section on cover letters.

DOs AND DON'Ts OF RÉSUMÉ WRITING

DOs

✓ Do list other languages you speak if you are going to be dealing with the public. Candidates with more than one language are an asset to companies and organizations because they can provide better customer service.

✓ Do list all the computer programs you know.

✓ Do have someone you trust proofread your résumé for spelling mistakes and grammar.

✓ Do use professional wording; for example, "childcare" sounds better than "baby-sitting."

✓ Do send a clean, neat, and tidy résumé.

DON'Ts

✗ Don't list your date of birth or your social insurance number or references.

✗ Don't attach a photograph of yourself unless it is specifically required.

✗ Don't print your résumé on coloured paper. Use only white, off-white, or light grey.

✗ Don't send a résumé that has been photocopied so many times that it is blurry or crooked on the page. Print a fresh copy that has been updated with your latest skills and experience.

✗ Don't ever lie, mislead, or inflate your actual skills and experience.

✗ Don't overdo fonts, boldface, underlining, or italics.

✗ Don't squish your résumé onto one page if you have enough to fill a second page. A second page is fine as long as you don't have too much white space left over at the bottom.

Sample résumés

The pages that follow contain several sample résumés. Take a good look at each of them and then decide which is most like the one you want to create for yourself. Work with it and make yours great and truly your own.

- See pages 40–42 for examples of the most common style of résumé for young people — the *combination résumé*. The first sample résumé is a blank outline you can use as a guide.
- See page 43 for an example of a *functional résumé*. It is a good style to choose if you have very little or no work experience, as it de-emphasizes work experience and education.
- See page 44 for an example of a *chronological résumé*. This is the traditional style of résumé that is best used if you have completed your education and have a solid work history over a few years.

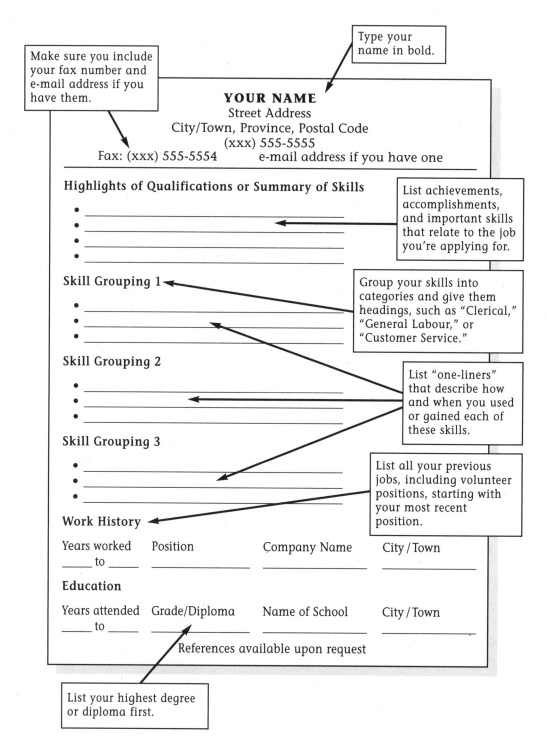

Type your name in bold.

Make sure you include your fax number and e-mail address if you have them.

YOUR NAME
Street Address
City/Town, Province, Postal Code
(xxx) 555-5555
Fax: (xxx) 555-5554   e-mail address if you have one

Highlights of Qualifications or Summary of Skills

- _____
- _____
- _____
- _____

List achievements, accomplishments, and important skills that relate to the job you're applying for.

Skill Grouping 1

- _____
- _____
- _____

Group your skills into categories and give them headings, such as "Clerical," "General Labour," or "Customer Service."

Skill Grouping 2

- _____
- _____
- _____

List "one-liners" that describe how and when you used or gained each of these skills.

Skill Grouping 3

- _____
- _____
- _____

List all your previous jobs, including volunteer positions, starting with your most recent position.

Work History

Years worked	Position	Company Name	City/Town
___ to ___	_____	_____	_____

Education

Years attended	Grade/Diploma	Name of School	City/Town
___ to ___	_____	_____	_____

References available upon request

List your highest degree or diploma first.

WILLIAM JACKSON
41 West Street
Toronto, Ontario
M5A 6L3
(416) 555-9286

HIGHLIGHTS OF QUALIFICATIONS OR SUMMARY OF SKILLS

- Trustworthy, responsible, reliable
- Works well with others or independently
- Able to complete tasks within limited time
- Committed employee
- Experience handling cash and cheque transactions
- Able to use a variety of landscaping equipment responsibly and safely

RELEVANT SKILLS AND ABILITIES

GENERAL LABOUR

- Operated gas-powered lawn mower and trimmer
- Loaded and unloaded equipment from truck
- Worked over sixty hours a week and maintained productivity
- Hauled away trimmings and debris

CUSTOMER SERVICE

- Maintained good relationships with clients by always being friendly and polite
- Helped company grow by asking clients for referrals
- Collected payments and issued receipts
- Called clients to verify that rain dates were convenient

WORK HISTORY

| 2004 to 2005 | Landscaper | Grasscutters | Toronto |
| 2003 to 2004 | Landscaper | J & T Landscaping | Toronto |

EDUCATION

| 2005 | Diploma | MacDonald Secondary School | Toronto |

References available upon request

JOANNA STEPHENS
723 Ellis Avenue
Halifax, Nova Scotia
B3J 6K2

(902) 555-2961   jstephens@freemail.com

HIGHLIGHTS OF QUALIFICATIONS OR SUMMARY OF SKILLS

COMPUTER LITERATE

- Able to work with minimal supervision
- Able to work as part of a team
- Excellent communication skills
- Professional and courteous

OFFICE SKILLS

- Answered phones on multi-line system
- Transferred calls to extensions or voice mailboxes
- Operated fax machine, photocopier, credit card authorization system
- Fast and accurate typing abilities
- Able to use a computer for word processing and data entry
- Performed light bookkeeping duties

CUSTOMER SERVICE SKILLS

- Worked at front desk and greeted people coming in
- Used polite phone manner
- Dealt with client complaints or directed them to appropriate person
- Promoted upcoming sales and/or events

WORK HISTORY

2004–present	data entry/back-up receptionist	MDL Systems Inc.	Halifax
2003–2004	cashier	Angie's Fashions	Halifax

EDUCATION

2002–2005	William Lyon MacKenzie S.S.	Halifax

References available upon request

RICHARD JONES
Box 23
Outlook, Saskatchewan S0L 2K3
(306) 555-1913

SUMMARY OF SKILLS

- Can do many tasks at once
- Committed to seeing things through
- Hardworking and dedicated
- Easily adapts to different environments
- Learns new tasks quickly

SKILLS & EXPERIENCES

GENERAL LABOUR

- Lifted over 60 lbs for extended periods of time
- Operated various types of farm equipment
- Performed building maintenance tasks: roof repair, caulking, eavestrough cleaning
- Interior and exterior painting

SALES

- Managed table at local farmers' market
- Set wages according to current prices
- Bartered effectively to attain best prices for goods
- Performed quality control checks on food being sold
- Gave proper change during cash transactions

ANIMAL CARE

- Tended to over 150 animals within limited time span (before school)
- Assisted with birthing of new pigs and sheep
- Since 1999, member of Youth 4-H
- Ensured safety of animals by proper fencing and gating

EDUCATION

2002 to present   Outlook High School, Outlook, Saskatchewan (to graduate 2006)

References available upon request

JENNIFER ALDERMAN
63 Westchester Street
Winnipeg, Manitoba R5T 2K4
(204) 555-4726

HIGHLIGHTS OF QUALIFICATIONS:

- Hardworking, honest, and reliable
- Experience dealing with children
- Good problem-solving skills
- Can do many things at once
- Good with people

RELEVANT EXPERIENCE:

2004–present   **Caregiver**
               Falcon Family, Winnipeg, MB

- Care for two children under the age of five without supervision
- Prepare meals and snacks
- Plan activities for children
- Supervise when friends come over to play

2003–2004   **Mother's Helper**
            Falcon Family, Winnipeg, MB

- Assisted with care of newborn baby — feeding, changing
- Played games with two-year-old while mother rested
- Made sure all toys were put away properly
- Taught two-year-old how to say the alphabet

EDUCATION:

2003–present   **Lester B. Pearson Secondary School**
               Winnipeg, MB
               - Expected date of graduation: Spring 2007

References available upon request

You finished your résumé! Great. But make sure you don't stop there. A very important thing to know about making a résumé is that once you get a general version finished, you should be prepared to change your résumé slightly for each different job you apply to. This is also true for cover letters. Employers will respond more favourably and this will greatly increase your chances of getting an interview.

Where to get more résumé help

Résumés can be difficult to write when you're starting out. Almost everyone, at some time in their life, has had to write a résumé. Ask around. Try a teacher, guidance counsellor, family member, or youth worker. Also, keep in mind that there are professionals at youth employment centres who can help you write your résumé. Most services are completely free. Check out Chapter 17 for help in finding a centre near you.

5

Cover Letters

"Do I always need a cover letter?"

This looks great

Writing a cover letter might seem like extra work, but remember — you want that job. A cover letter is a chance to make a good first impression. It's the first small step to showing an employer that . . .

- you're the best person for the job
- you can do the job
- you want the job.

It will never, ever *hurt* you to write a cover letter. Employers will rarely say in an ad, or in person, "Be sure to write a cover letter." That's because it's expected of you. "Drop off your résumé" always means that you should also attach a cover letter. A good cover letter will give you an edge over the other applicants.

Cover letters and résumés are different. They can tell the employer different things about you. Think of a cover letter as a very short advertisement or commercial for yourself. It does not just repeat what is on your résumé. A cover letter introduces you and your résumé, and it's an opportunity to state your strongest points and show an employer why you are the right person for the job.

What is a cover letter?

A cover letter is a professional-looking business letter, written with a personal touch, that is meant to "cover," or accompany, your résumé. You use a cover letter to tell an employer things like how and why you are a quick learner, friendly, helpful, and trustworthy, preferably by giving examples of when you showed these skills.

The good news is that your cover letter should be short. It will contain only three or four paragraphs and should not be more than one page long.

TIP If you have little or no work experience, your cover letter can contain as few as two short paragraphs.

Keep in mind that a cover letter is often your first introduction to an employer. First impressions count for a lot, so your cover letter must be a strong, sincere, honest, and clear statement about yourself, your intentions, and your abilities.

Why cover letters can make a difference

A cover letter is an important part of applying for almost any job. At a glance, it tells an employer . . .

- which job you want
- that you have the necessary skills and qualifications

- that you want to work for their company or organization
- how and where to contact you for an interview.

The job I'm applying for has an application form. Do I still have to write a cover letter?

No, it's not essential, but it's strongly advised. Going to the trouble of writing a cover letter may give you the edge over other candidates and get you an interview.

TIP Make the best impression you can. Whenever you hand in an application form you should also attach your résumé and a cover letter.

Do I need a cover letter when I'm applying for part-time or summer jobs?

Yes. It doesn't matter if you are applying for an entry-level full-time, part-time, or summer job, you will always need a cover letter.

I'm applying for so many jobs — can I re-use my cover letter?

No, that's not a great idea. Each job that you apply for will require a new, customized cover letter.

The good news is that once you have done one they get much easier and quicker to write. This is especially true if you are applying for several jobs of the same type. It's important to look carefully at the position you want and write your cover letter for that specific position. All jobs are different and require their own cover letters. Taking the time to write your letter for each job will help you get interviews.

LOOK AT IT FROM THE EMPLOYER'S POINT OF VIEW

An employer uses your cover letter as one more way to choose between you and other applicants. Many employers receive hundreds of applications and résumés. When there is a lot of competition for a job, a strong cover letter may be what sets you apart.

Who is it addressed to?

Before you begin, find out who you should send your application to and address your letter to that person. Use the person's name (make sure you've spelled it correctly) and title as given in the advertisement. If there is not a specific person listed, or if you are dropping off your résumé to an employer that has not specifically advertised a position, try to find out who will be doing the hiring. You can do this by phoning the employer first. Often the person who answers the phone can help you. It's easy. All you need to say is something like:

- "Hello. My name is _____ _____ . Could you tell me the name of the person in charge of hiring the summer staff?"
  or
- "Good morning. I'm applying for the part-time position that is posted in your window. Can you please tell me the name of the person I should address my application to?"
  or
- "Hello. I'm applying for the _____ position advertised in the newspaper yesterday. Could you please tell me who I should address my cover letter to?"

Be sure to ask for the correct spelling, and the person's title.

If you can't call to find out a name because the advertisement specifically requests "no phone calls, please," you will have to address your letter in general terms. For example, you can start your letter with "Dear Sir or Madam," "Dear Hiring Manager," or "Dear Selection Committee."

It's always best to have the correct person's name, so try to obtain it whenever possible. Going to the extra trouble always makes a good impression.

How do I set up my cover letter?

At the top of the letter, include your personal information:

- your name
- your address
- your phone number
- your e-mail address (if you have one, and you check it regularly)

Next, two lines down, comes the date. Then, two lines later, add the employer information:

- the hiring manager's name
- the hiring manager's title (e.g., Manager, Director of Human Resources, Owner)
- the full company name
- the company's address

Check out the samples on pages 58–61.

The three main parts of a cover letter

The opening

Remember, a cover letter should be short — no longer than one page — and will probably only contain only three or four paragraphs.

In the opening paragraph, state which position you are applying for (remember to quote a position number if the advertisement listed one) and where and when the position was advertised. If the job was not advertised in a newspaper or on a website, be sure to say where and how you heard of the opening. Perhaps someone mentioned the position to you, or you saw a sign in a window, or picked up an application and information package at a job fair.

The middle

In the body of your letter, write one, two, or three short paragraphs that describe any of your skills, experience, or qualifications that directly relate to the position you are applying for. Mention the most important and most relevant items first. Don't repeat everything your résumé says. Just pick one or two specific experiences or achievements and relate them to the position you want.

If you haven't done this type of job before, or a similar type of job, it's okay to tell the employer. Let them know that you really want the job. Tell them you are a hard worker and give them an example of when you demonstrated this in another job, or at school, or on a sports team, or in a hobby. Explain to the employer that you are a quick learner and also give an example. List your personal strengths and qualities. Last, tell them that you'd really like to work for their company and say why.

The end

The closing paragraph should summarize why you are an excellent candidate and where you can be reached. Be clear, firm, and confident, but avoid overly emotional statements that seem needy or desperate.

What if I don't have any experience at all?

If this is your first job, or you do not feel you have enough experience that relates to the position, you're not alone. Everyone has doubts. But before you give up, take another look at your résumé. Re-read what is there and remind yourself of all the things you've done and all the things that make you a good and special person. What would your friends say about you? Now, think about the job you're applying for. Ask yourself: what qualities do I have that the employer will be looking for?

Another way to discover your relevant experience is to look closely at the advertisement or job posting. Often an ad tells you exactly what the employer wants to hear in a cover letter. Look for what comes after key phrases like: "The successful candidate will have . . ." or "If you are . . ."

Also, consider what it would be like to do the job. What qualities might the employer need in an employee? If you want to work in retail, where you have to handle cash and stock, then attributes like "honesty" and "trustworthiness" are important. So when you look back at your previous jobs, volunteer work, school activities, hobbies, sports, or extra-curricular activities, can you think of times when you demonstrated "honesty" or "trustworthiness"?

The trick is to match your own experiences, and the qualities they demonstrate in you, with what the employer will require of a successful candidate.

Here are some examples of the qualities employers tend to look for in an employee, matched up with common experiences:

EXPERIENCES	QUALITIES EMPLOYERS LOOK FOR
Sport	
played on a sporting team	team player, outgoing, motivated, driven
coached a kids team	a leader, reliable, trustworthy
Extra-curricular	
performed in a play	creative, able to speak in front of groups
play chess	able to concentrate, attentive to detail
play musical instruments	creative, dedicated, focused
At School	
strong at science	inquisitive, able to solve problems
strong at math	analytical, logical
strong at English	good at writing, communicating
strong at gym	physically strong, team player, dedicated
Volunteer Work	
helped at seniors home	sensitive, kind
worked with disabled	patient, caring
Previous Positions	
baby-sitter	trustworthy, flexible, calm, responsible
lifeguard	energetic, serious, independent

Match up your own experiences with the employer's needs. Put them in the body of your cover letter. Tell the employer you are capable of doing a great job because of your personal qualities. And always give supporting examples when you can.

How should it look? What style?

Your cover letter must be on either standard plain white, off-white, or very light grey 8 ½" × 11" paper. Always type your cover letter. If you don't have a computer, ask a friend if you can use theirs. Do not write it by hand. Use the same font style and size as your résumé. Single-space your cover letter, keeping a double space between paragraphs.

Be sure to spellcheck your letter, and have someone you trust read it over to make sure you don't have any spelling or grammar mistakes.

How should I send my cover letter?

If you are responding to an advertisement that states exactly how the employer wishes to receive your application, then always follow those instructions.

If it's left up to you, or you are responding to a "help wanted" sign or a lead from a friend, or you are taking initiative and simply forwarding your résumé, then follow these basic guidelines:

In person

For entry-level positions, it's always best to drop off your application in person. This way you'll be sure it arrives safely, and it gives you another opportunity to make a good impression. If it's possible, hand your application to the hiring manager personally. Remember to smile and dress neatly. You will also be able to see the company with your own eyes. Often you can pick up some information on the company at the reception desk. Read it carefully; it could be useful if you get an interview. You may feel intimidated or shy about just walking into a strange office. Everyone does — it's natural. But the more you do it, the easier it gets, and best of all, taking this kind of action will raise your confidence level and help you get that interview.

By fax

If an ad asks you to fax your application, then be sure to do a separate fax cover sheet. A fax cover sheet is like a title page. A typical one looks like the

---

FAX COVER PAGE

From: Your name
Fax number: (416) 555-5555
Phone number: (416) 555-1234

Date: April 10, 2005

To: Mr. John Smith
Fax number: (416) 555-4444

Number of pages, including this cover: 4

---

sample on the previous page. Somewhere on the page (either at the very top or the very bottom) you should also include your address, your phone number, your fax number (if you have one), and your e-mail address.

By regular mail

If you are mailing in your application, use a large (9" x 12") envelope so you do not have to fold your résumé and cover letter. If your résumé is two pages long, staple the pages together. Attach your cover letter (and the application form, if there is one) to your résumé with a paper clip. Be sure to go to the post office and buy the correct postage for the envelope — it costs more to mail a large envelope than it does to mail a regular letter.

By e-mail

If you are asked to e-mail your application, make sure you know how to send an attachment. If you're not sure how, have someone help you. It's a good idea to include your name and phone number in the body of your e-mail message so the employer will know how to contact you if your attachment doesn't work. This does occasionally happen. So, try to send a simple or text-only version of your attachment as well as your normal copy. This way, even if the employer is using older software and can't open the formatted version of your attachment, the basic information in your résumé and cover letter will still be clear.

Remember, sending a cover letter and résumé by e-mail shows that you know how to use your computer. But it will only impress an employer if you do it correctly. If you have any questions, ask a friend or teacher to help you.

DOs AND DON'Ts OF COVER LETTERS

DOs

✓ Do have an answering machine or voice mail at the phone number you provide in your letter.

✓ Do tell friends or family members to take detailed messages for you while you are job searching.

✓ Do use an e-mail address that is proper (avoid nicknames or slang) and be sure you check your e-mail often during your job search.

✓ Do have someone you trust (teacher, parent, friend, employment counsellor) proofread your cover letter. Poor grammar and spelling mistakes are unprofessional. Take the extra time to ensure they are avoided. Write a new cover letter for every job you apply for.

DON'Ts

✗ Don't say how much you want to be paid in your cover letter, unless an advertisement asks you to give a salary expectation.

✗ Don't put your references in your cover letter.

✗ Don't rush your letter. After you've written it, wait a day, then look at it again with a fresh perspective.

✗ Don't forget to sign your letter in blue or black pen.

✗ Don't oversell yourself. It's important to be confident, but don't overdo it.

CHECKLIST — THE COVER LETTER

- My phone number is on my cover letter.
- I have voice mail or an answering machine at the phone number I'm using and the outgoing message is straightforward and professional.
- I have the correct spelling of the hiring manager's name.
- If there is a position number or title, I have quoted it in my letter.
- In the body of my letter, I have included my most relevant experience first.
- I have said some positive things about myself that relate to the job.
- I have spellchecked my letter and had someone I trust read it over for errors.
- I have signed my letter.

Sample cover letters

To get you started, on pages 58–61 are four examples of great cover letters for first jobs. You can follow them as examples, but don't just copy them. Be yourself. There is no "perfect" or "right" cover letter because everyone is different. Make your cover letters reflect who you are, what you can do and offer, and what you enjoy.

- See page 58 for an example of a cover letter for a job similar to one the applicant has had before. (Applicant: Jacob Poulos)

- See page 59 for an example of a cover letter for when the applicant has relevant experience, but it's not an exact match for the position. (Applicant: Emma Cho)

- See page 60 for a cover letter for a situation in which the applicant's experience is not related to the job being applied for. (Applicant: Mohammed Akil)

- See page 61 for a great sample cover letter for when the applicant has no *direct* experience but the experience they do have is indirectly related to the job being applied for. (Applicant: Jesse Brown)

I still need more help with my cover letter . . .

Cover letters can sometimes be difficult to write, especially if it's your first time. Lots of people can help you. Just remember, among your parents, teachers, friends, and siblings you will be able to find someone who has written a cover letter at some point in their life. Ask them to give you a hand. Also, there are many places to go to get cover letter help from professionals — and most services for youth are free. Check out Chapter 17 of this book for help in finding a centre near you.

JACOB POULOS
12 King Street,
Victoria, BC V1W 1A1
(250) 555-3333
jacobp@internet.com

April 10, 2005

Ms. Jennifer Burton
Day Camp Director
Camp Wannabe
222 Lions Bridge Rd.,
Suite 201,
Victoria, BC V2R 3Y2

Dear Ms. Burton:

RE: Junior Day Camp Counsellor

I wish to apply for the position of Junior Day Camp Counsellor at Camp Wannabe as advertised on a flyer in the guidance office at my high school.

I love summer camp. Until last year, I spent a month of every summer as a camper at Camp Lotsafun, a residential camp for kids. Over my years there I learned over 100 camp songs. During my last summer as a Counsellor in Training, I learned how to set an example for the younger campers and to be a positive role model. I was often responsible for planning and leading games and crafts activities. Being a leader was a great learning opportunity for me. I developed a strong sense of responsibility — something every counsellor needs.

As you can see from my attached résumé, I will be finishing grade 10 in June and would be available to work all summer, full-time. I think I would make an excellent day camp counsellor and I look forward to hearing from you about an interview. My telephone number is (250) 555-3333.

Sincerely,

Jacob Poulos

Jacob Poulos

EMMA CHO

4667–413 22nd Ave.,

Edmonton, AB T6K 1Z2

(403) 555-7890

Emma@theweb.ca

January 10, 2005

Dr. Eva Night
2 South St.,
Edmonton, AB T5L 4A3

Dear Dr. Night:

At my friend Scott Smith's last appointment, you mentioned that you would be needing some extra reception help in your office soon. He was kind enough to pass this information on to me. If this is still the case, I would like to offer my services.

For the past three months I have been working part-time, three evenings per week, as a telemarketer at ABC Corp., downtown. Talking with up to fifty customers per evening, I have gained a great deal of customer service experience. I am confident on the phone and I also have basic computer skills.

Attached is my résumé. I would be available to work part-time weekdays. I have always thought of doctors' offices as friendly environments and so I know I would enjoy working with you. I hope to hear from you soon.

Sincerely,

Emma Cho

Emma Cho

MOHAMMED AKIL

345 Dunberry Lane,

Toronto, ON M5E 2I7

(416) 555-6178

April 11, 2005

Andrea Klauss
Manager, Downtown Cinemas
2789 Main Street
Toronto, ON M8R 2K5

Dear Andrea Klauss,

Please accept my résumé as application for the Downtown Cinemas Box Office Attendant position advertised by the Help Wanted sign you have posted. I am very excited about possibly joining your team.

As someone who goes to see movies all the time, I know what it takes to be a good box office attendant. I am polite and friendly and I know I would be a good representative for Downtown Cinemas. From my experience playing on many different sports teams at my school, I know I will get along well with my co-workers, and can always be relied upon to help out when I'm needed. Please call me at my home number, (416) 555-6178, to arrange a time when I can come in and speak with you. My family or voice mail will take a message for me if I am not in. I go to school from Monday to Friday between 9:00 a.m. and 3:45 p.m. but I would be free any other time. Thank you for your consideration.

Sincerely,

Mohammed Akil

JESSE BROWN

36 Custer St.,
Vancouver, BC V6K 2K8
Tel: (604) 555-1175

May 22, 2005

Felix Katz
Manager, CD Emporium
420 McDonald Ave., Suite 102
Vancouver, BC V3T 5K7

Dear Mr. Katz,

I came into the store yesterday and spoke to Josh, who suggested that if I was interested in submitting my résumé, you would keep it on file. I would like to be considered for any position that becomes available.

I have been to your store many times and it seems like a really great place to work. I am hardworking and responsible and I get along well with people. I know you probably prefer to hire people with retail experience, but in my case I think you should make an exception.

As you can see on my résumé, I love music. I love to play music, listen to music, and someday I would like to write music. I am so enthusiastic about all types of music that I know I would be a great person to help people buy CDs. I realize I would have a lot to learn, but I also feel I already have a lot to offer.

I would love a chance to come in to talk to you in person. I will call you Friday afternoon to arrange a time for us to meet. If it is easier for you, please feel free to contact me at my home number, (604) 555-1175. Thank you for your time.

Sincerely,

Jesse Brown

Jesse Brown

6

Job Searching

"Where are all the jobs?"

Did you know that many jobs, especially entry-level jobs, are never advertised in newspapers? This surprises most people. How, you might ask, can I find out about a job if it's not advertised somewhere? This chapter will help you discover all the different ways you can find out about positions that are available, and give you advice on how to apply for them. Job searching takes time and effort, but if you stick with it, you will succeed.

What's the very first thing I should do?

Before you do anything else, it's a great idea to tell everyone you know that you are looking for a job. Tell them to tell people they know. This is called networking.

How can I network?

Networking is an excellent way to let job leads come to you. It will be more important to your chances of getting a job than anything else you do.

Take a few hours and call everyone you can think of and say something like this:

- "Hi, it's (your name). I just wanted to give you a quick call. I'm looking for a (summer/part-time/full-time) job. So I'm calling everyone I can to let them know I'm looking. I'm interested in (types of jobs). If you hear of anything at all can you let me know? I'd really appreciate any help you can give me. Thanks very much."

Or send e-mails to your friends, relatives, and any other contacts you know who might be able to help you find a job. Keep your e-mail short and to the point, and be sure to thank the people for their time.

FACT Many young people get their first few jobs through connections. Parents, teachers, siblings, friends, parents of friends, aunts and uncles, neighbours, and coaches are all excellent sources of information about job openings.

It's important to tell people what kind of job you are looking for and what special skills you have to offer. Remember, networking is not asking for a job. Networking is making connections with people you already know and asking them to keep their eye out for suitable positions for you. The more people you tell, the better your chances will be.

Does networking work?

Try this: think about how fast rumours spread. Now imagine if you could use this for good, to help you get a job! That's kind of what networking does. It uses the power of association to help you get what you want: a job. Remember to thank people for "keeping their eye out for a job for you," and now that you are a part of their network, be prepared for them to ask you to return the favour sometime.

What if "networking" just isn't done in my culture?

There's no need to feel shy or ashamed about asking friends and family to keep you in mind as they hear about jobs. In some cultures, of course, networking isn't done. But in Canada networking is very common and people do it when they're looking for all kinds of things like an apartment, a used car, a good restaurant or music store, even a new dentist. Make sure you explain this to any friends or family who are newer to Canada and don't understand why you are asking them to help you look for a job.

TRUE STORIES

Being in the Right Place at the Right Time

- Anna heard about her job from her sister, Jennie. Jennie was speaking with her boyfriend's mother, Carol. At Carol's shop they needed a part-time person right away because someone had just quit and it was getting close to Christmas. Later, Jennie told this to Anna, and Anna called Carol. Anna had an interview the next day. She got the job right away.

- Troy's uncle Gus works in a factory. Gus heard from his boss Peta that the front office would soon be hiring for an entry-level position. Did he know a young person who was looking for a job? No, he said. Then, luckily, Troy called Gus to tell him he was looking for a job. "Well, you've got great timing, young man," said Gus. "I think we're hiring. Call me at work tomorrow. I'll put you through to the boss, Peta." Troy got the job the next week.

TIP Remember to thank the person who helps you find a job. You never know when you might need their help again. Everyone likes to be appreciated.

Where should I start looking?

After you have begun to network with as many people as you can think of, it's time to try the other routes.

TIP Act on a good lead right away. The sooner you make that phone call, the greater the chances that you'll be ahead of someone else.

Classifieds: how to read job ads

In most newspapers, the classified section is still a good source of job openings. This is especially true if you are looking for full-time or part-time work. Generally speaking, classifieds are not as good for summer jobs, although many do carry some summer jobs or "seasonal" postings during the summer months.

Looking in the classifieds takes patience. In big cities, there may be as many as five newspapers to look through. Be sure to check out the major daily papers, as well as the free weekly newspapers, as these also have job listings. You will soon get to know which papers in your area carry the kinds of jobs you are looking for and on which days they run. This makes it easier and less time-consuming.

Keep in mind how many other people also look through the classifieds. You've got a lot of competition, so don't let it be the only way you look for jobs.

Classified tips

- Always circle an interesting ad when you see it and keep going. Come back to the circled ones at the end.
- Look through the ads in the morning. Sometimes jobs fill quickly and the afternoon might be too late.
- Most libraries and employment centres have free newspapers for you to look through.
- Read the ad you're interested in many times. Make sure you have the skills and qualifications they are looking for.

Spotting classified "scams"

Be very wary of classified ads that sound too good to be true. If an ad promises to pay you beyond your wildest dreams and says "no experience necessary," or "Hey Students! Make $1,000 per week," it means there is probably a catch, and it might be a scam.

> TIP Scam warning Never pay an employer your own money before you start a job. You should not have to pay for the products you are going to sell. Don't sign a sales contract without having someone you trust, like a parent, teacher, or friend, review it first.

Why are there so many sales ads in the classified section?

Many young people work in sales jobs, whether that means working in a retail shop, telemarketing, or selling things door to door. Sales jobs can be very exciting and fast-paced, and will often pay quite well, especially if you are good at selling. But beware! One of the reasons there seem to be so many sales jobs advertised is because selling can be really tough, and the way you get paid (for example, by commission) is often not very secure or reliable. So before you accept a job offer, make sure you know what's involved. For more about sales jobs, commissions, and base pay, see pages 112–13.

TIP It's easier to sell something that you yourself believe in, use, or think is a good product or service.

What is the "hidden job market"?

The "hidden job market" is a term that refers to the many jobs that are never advertised in the newspapers. Companies and organizations, especially smaller ones, often rely on internal postings and word of mouth to attract potential candidates.

How do I tap into the hidden job market?

Here are some of the ways you can reach jobs in the hidden job market:

- networking
- applying in person to discover unadvertised jobs
- seeking out free employment programs and services
- searching on the Internet
- attending job fairs and visiting job banks
- conducting information interviews
- self-advertising
- cold calling

Applying in person

A common and successful way to look for a job is by applying in person. In fact, for some industries, such as retail and restaurants, employers often prefer that you apply in person. When you go, have a stack of résumés with you, but be prepared to pick up an application

form (see Chapter 3) too. (And remember to follow the Ten Steps to a Successful Application Form listed on pages 22–25.)

Free programs and services

Many communities in Canada have employment services specifically geared toward youth. Read Chapter 17 to see how you can find such a service in your own town or city, or contact your province's ministry of labour by visiting their website or looking them up in the government listings (the "blue pages") of the phone book. You can also try looking up "employment" in your local phone book or Yellow Pages.

The main benefit of *youth* employment centres is that, compared with other employment agencies, they are specially equipped to help young people find jobs. Many also have access to jobs that are not advertised elsewhere and are reserved especially for young people. It's definitely worth giving one a call.

Finding jobs online

The Internet is changing the way we communicate with one another. Information and news that used to take days or even weeks to get to someone now takes minutes or seconds to reach people around the world. Using more tools will give your job search more power, and the Internet offers many ways to help you search.

INTERNET JOB-SEARCH RESOURCES INCLUDE . . .

- job postings
- résumé postings
- job-search assistance
- information on potential employers, occupations, and industries
- access to people who can help you to succeed
- telephone and business directories
- maps to interviews
- job alerts for jobs that match your interests

Where do I go online to find the jobs I want?

Why bother using the Internet to search for a job?

- The Internet is open 24/7. So if you want to look for job postings before you leave the house in the morning, or late at night when things are quiet, you can.
- Using the Internet shows the employer that you have computer skills.
- The Internet can help you explore jobs and options you never thought about. Not sure what a sous-chef does? Look it up! What sounds like fun? Check it out online! You can also find online self-assessment tools, tons of different types of jobs, and even lists of local career counsellors and career centres to help if you feel you need it.
- The Internet allows you to check for jobs on company websites and job banks in seconds. You can use search engines to discover what jobs are available, and to sign up for job alerts so that you'll be the first to know about it when the job of your dreams becomes open.

WHAT IS A . . .

- **database?** A database is any organized collection of information, such as a telephone book or the files on your computer; online employment databases store information about available jobs.
- **job bank?** An Internet job bank is an electronic listing of jobs, work, or business opportunities provided by a broad range of employers.
- **job search engine?** A job search engine is an electronic tool used to search for a job using different categories such as location, job title, and job description to find what you're looking for.

What if I don't have a computer at home?

If you don't have a computer at home, or if your computer isn't fast enough to do good Internet searches, you can get access from other places, such as youth employment centres, libraries, employment resource centres, a friend's house, or a school or college computer lab.

Should I create my own e-mail address?

Yes, and make sure it's a proper e-mail address for a job search. A potential employer will not mind if your email is jsmith@email.com, but an address like cutiepie@email.com may not create the most professional impression. Make sure your e-mail address reflects the image you want the person doing the hiring to see.

DOs AND DON'Ts OF ELECTRONIC COMMUNICATION

DOs

✓ Do keep messages short.

✓ Do check for proper spelling, grammar, and punctuation.

✓ Do say exactly what you mean.

✓ Do be courteous and professional.

✓ Do send cover letters and résumés in the format an employer requests.

DON'Ts

✗ Don't USE ALL CAPITAL LETTERS — in an electronic environment, this is the same as shouting.

✗ Don't add emoticons :-)

✗ Don't use acronyms or other short forms.

✗ Don't use clever or silly e-mail addresses — keep it simple.

What other Internet resources can I use?

Besides job search engines and databases, many good resources are available on the web for your job search. Online versions of newspapers and magazines often give you the option of narrowing down your search of their job ads. You can also check out other websites, such as the sites for youth employment centres, libraries, community organizations, associations, and university and college career planning offices. Many websites have a link for upcoming job opportunities. Sometimes the information is listed in the "Contact Us" section. Surf around until you can find out more. Often the website will not only show you what jobs are available, but will also tell you how the employer prefers to receive résumés and if they accept phone calls about employment. Always follow the instructions on the job posting. If an employer wants résumés only by e-mail or fax, don't send in your résumé by mail or in person.

TIP Searching for a job on the Internet is not the same as surfing the Internet for fun. You should dedicate a certain amount of time specifically to your job search. If you come across something fun in your search, bookmark the site so you can return to it later.

Can the Internet help me find out about different companies and organizations?

If you've made up your mind to apply for a job with a particular company, the web is a good place to learn about that company. On its website a company or organization will usually give you a summary of the products and services it offers, as well as a listing of the people who work there. You can use this information to learn who to direct your cover letter to, to prepare for an interview, or simply to figure out whether this company would be a good place for you to work.

TIP You can also search by organization or institution for a job. For example, if you want a job at IBM or the Toronto Public Library, you can go to their websites directly to see what's available and how they accept résumés.

What if I'm moving? Can I look for a job in another city or province?

The Internet has made it easy to look for a job in another part of Canada. If you are moving, or you're spending your summer somewhere else, you can search for jobs in Toronto from Halifax. You can send in your résumé for a job in Ottawa from Whitehorse.

Many job banks will let you search for jobs in specific cities or regions, and will alert you to postings for jobs in places you have selected. This saves you time that you would otherwise spend sifting through postings. Be prepared to travel for an interview, and make certain that you have the time and money to do so.

Is any job search database complete?

No. Remember that no one database has every single job listing. You should search on many different sites to get a more comprehensive list of what's available. Chapter 17 lists several job search websites that you can use in your search.

TIP Many job search engines allow you to sign up for job alerts. When a job in your area of interest and level of experience comes up on the website, the site will automatically e-mail you with a notice of the posting.

How accurate is the information on the web?

A lot of the information on the Internet is accurate and up-to-date; however, you should always consider the source. If someone from a newsgroup you're on directs you to a brand new website with great job leads, the site might seem very cool, but you should try to look for ways to check the information. Ask who made the website, whether the posting is recent, and when the website was last updated. You can usually see when a webpage was last updated on the opening page, or at the bottom of any page, depending on the designer. Also, it's a good idea to look for other sources that confirm the information you've found.

TIP Not all websites are created equal. You'll find that some websites are great in helping you find the information you need to help you find a job. Others are not so great. Bookmark interesting websites you find in your travels so you can return to them later.

Wow, the Internet is full of information. Why do I need to look anywhere else for a job?

While the Internet is a good tool, it is only one of a variety of tools and strategies you should use in your search for a job. Different employers will post jobs in different places.

Some employers post all jobs in Internet job banks, others post information only on their own websites, and others may ignore the Internet entirely and post jobs in the windows of their businesses, in newspapers, or at employment centres.

Many employers don't post vacancies at all. They might tell their current staff to let others know about an opening. Others take applications all year round, so that when they have an opening they already have interested people.

Using only one tool may cause you to miss the perfect posting in another place. A good job search includes a combination of strategies, including pen and paper applications, paper résumés, direct contact with potential employers, networking, interviewing, and the Internet. Technology may give you an edge over your competitor who doesn't have access to the Internet, but it is not the only way to do a successful job search.

WARNING You might get a call from someone who found your résumé online and would like to schedule an interview with you. Even if they don't sound strange, always ask for a contact number or e-mail, the name of the company, the type of position they're offering, and if the company has a website. Research the company, and if you don't feel comfortable that the business is legitimate, then call or e-mail to cancel, or to get more information. It's better to be safe than sorry.

Can I send my résumé via e-mail?

Yes, you can e-mail your résumé to an employer if the employer accepts e-mail résumés. If you are responding to a job posting, follow the instructions for how to submit a résumé to the letter. If an employer asks you to send your résumé as an attachment in a specific file format, make certain that you send it in that format. You can use the body of the e-mail as a brief cover letter, stating where you found the job and why you're interested in working for the company, and inviting the reader to get in touch with you.

Remember, an e-mail cover letter is still a cover letter — do everything you would do in a regular letter, including checking spelling, using standard language and punctuation, and "signing" your full name at the end. For more information on how to write your résumé and cover letter, read Chapters 4 and 5.

WHAT IS A . . .

- **plain-text résumé?** A résumé pasted into the body of an e-mail, without any fancy formatting, bold, italics, or interesting layout.
- **online application form?** A website that has fields for the information the employer needs to consider you for a job.
- **.rtf attachment?** A file saved in "rich text format," a file format that many different word processing programs can read. Files saved as .rtf files may lose some of the fancy formatting, so it's a good idea to make your e-résumé as simple as possible.

Regardless of your cover e-mail's file format, it should include the same elements as the paper cover letter described in Chapter 5. An employer wants to know where you found the information about the job or the company, why you want to work for the company, and why you think you're a good fit for the company. Even though e-mail is less formal than a paper letter, you still need to sound respectful.

Who should I e-mail my résumé to?

If you're responding to a job ad, send your résumé directly to the address given in the ad. If you don't know who to address your cover e-mail to, try searching the company website to find out who does the hiring. Does the company have its own HR department? If so, you can address your letter to the HR Manager. Make sure you spell the person's name correctly. If you don't come up with a name in your search, you may use "To Whom It May Concern," or "Dear Sir/Madam."

Job fairs

At job fairs, a number of employers who are hiring come together and set up booths to talk directly to job searchers. They are often held in halls, schools, malls, hotels, conference centres, arenas, or employment centres. They are a great way to meet potential employers face to face, fill out applications, submit your résumé, and learn about different companies and organizations. Sometimes they even have on-the-spot interviews — so be prepared. When you go, look your best and be sure to bring along copies of your résumé so you can take full advantage of the event.

TIP   Remember to dress neatly and be very polite when you attend a job fair. Make a good impression on potential employers. Also, keep track of the names of the employers to whom you've handed in your résumés. Take every opportunity to talk with employers. The more practice you get, the easier you will find interviews.

What's an internal posting?

A position is "posted internally" when it is advertised only within the company that is doing the hiring. Employers may post the job on the company bulletin board, send a notice around in an e-mail message, or simply ask their employees to encourage anyone they know who might be qualified to call for more information. Companies and organizations save money on advertising this way. They also benefit because the candidates often come recommended by someone already on staff.

The only way to hear about internal postings is to network. You never know who may help you. Tell as many people as you can that you are looking for a job so someone will think of you when an internal posting becomes available.

Information interviews

A great way to introduce yourself to an employer is to ask for an information interview. This is becoming a very common tool for young people, especially those who are trying to break into a specific field of interest.

If you have your sights set on a particular career, industry, or field and you need to learn more about it, then one way is to call or e-mail someone who already works in that field and ask for an information interview. Ask around. See if your parents, friends, or other acquaintances know someone in the field you are interested in. They may be able to help you set up an information interview. It may be that you'll need to make a "cold call" to someone who doesn't know you. See pages 79–82 for more information and tips on how to make these kinds of calls.

When it comes time to conduct an information interview, it is important to be well prepared. You should have a list of questions written out and take notes. Keep your questions short, as the person's time is valuable, and even though you are not applying for a job right now, you might one day meet again. So, it's important that you leave the person with a good impression.

Information interviews offer an opportunity for you to learn about what it takes to break into your field of interest. Here are some of the things you should ask about:

- What are the typical educational requirements?
- Where do most people obtain these qualifications?
- What does a typical day look like for the person you're interviewing? What would they recommend you do to get into the field?
- How did they break into the field?
- What other tips can the person give you?
- Could the person recommend anyone else you should talk to?
- Are there any good books or articles that you should read to research the field?

Someone who already works in a field that you wish to enter can be a great contact in years to come. You never know how, or when, that person may help you. Be polite, enthusiastic, and very thankful for their time.

Internships and co-op placements

Many organizations and companies work hand in hand with schools, colleges, and universities to provide internship and co-op positions. These are full-time or part-time positions that typically last for a few months of the year and add to your classroom learning by giving you on-the-job experience and school credits. Although they don't pay much, and sometimes nothing at all, they are an excellent way to learn about an industry, make contacts, and ultimately land a job. Companies do tend to hire interns or co-op students over other applicants because they already know the company and how it works — and they've already proven themselves to be good workers and right for the position.

In some industries, especially media-based ones, an internship is fast becoming the only way to break into the industry. Almost no entry-level jobs are advertised in the arts industries like film, TV, publishing, newspaper, graphic design, and multi-media industries, as they are always filled by co-op students and interns. To find out more about how you can become an intern or co-op student, call your local community college or set up an information interview with someone in the field.

Volunteering

One of the best ways to gain valuable on-the-job experience is to volunteer for a non-profit organization, a charity, or a person you know who is in need. You'll be doing good in your community. This, more than anything else, is what employers like to see in a potential employee. Someone who cares about others is the kind of person most employers want to hire.

Although you won't get paid to volunteer, the experience you'll gain is also a great reason to volunteer, especially if you haven't worked before, or you don't have a lot of work experience. A volunteer position is a great addition to your résumé. Like a paying job, it tells an employer that you made a commitment, stuck it out, and were successful. The person who supervised you at your volunteer job is also a good person to obtain a reference from.

FACT You might be thinking that volunteering is like working for nothing. It's not. Volunteering is a great way to meet people, learn on-the-job skills, and network. Many people get jobs while they are volunteering because they are in the right place at the right time.

Treat volunteering like a real job. Be reliable, prompt, and friendly. When you show this attitude, the people you are working with will want you to succeed. And they will want to help you get a paid job.

Getting a volunteer job takes time and a little effort. There may be a volunteer centre in your community that can help you. Check out your local phone book or www.volunteer.ca for a centre near you.

Apprenticeships

A growing number of young Canadians are exploring the option of doing an apprenticeship. This is a great way to learn the skills needed to enter a skilled trade — and to earn money while you do it. Talk to your guidance counsellor if you are at school, or to an employment counsellor, or call your province's ministry in charge of training. There are well over one hundred different trades that offer apprenticeships and let you earn while you learn. After you've finished being trained, many of these jobs are very well paid. There are hundreds of career options to discover.

Self-advertising

One way of getting employment is to advertise yourself. This is especially effective if you are offering a service such as baby-sitting, lawn mowing, raking leaves, designing websites, house painting, or doing odd jobs. There are many inexpensive ways to advertise yourself, from posting flyers and placing ads in your local papers, to making direct contact by phone, fax, or e-mail.

TIP Remember your own personal safety. If you are going out on a job, make sure you tell someone the address and phone number of where you are going.

Cold calling

Cold calling simply means picking up the phone and calling someone you don't know to gather information for your job search.

Cold calling is a great way to . . .

- get information about possible job leads
- introduce yourself to a potential employer and tell them about your skills and interests
- find out if an employer is hiring soon
- set up an information interview
- gain the kind of confidence you'll need to succeed in an interview.

Yes, in the beginning it takes a while to get up the nerve to make a cold call. While some people don't mind just calling someone out of the blue, for others it takes a while to gain the confidence.

But once you've done it a few times, you'll find it's easy. It's just talking on the phone, right? You do that all the time.

How do I find out who to call, and how do I get their phone number?

There are many ways to find the names and phone numbers of potential employers:

- Check out your local phone book or Yellow Pages if you know what kinds of employers or places you're looking for.
- Some employment books are also good sources of information on companies. For example, *The Canada Student Employment Guide*, which is published each year, lists which companies across Canada hire students and tells you what they look for.
- Business directories are big books that list businesses by location, product, or service. You can find them in your local Human Resources Centre of Canada, employment resource centre, or library.
- The Internet is a great source of company information. A company's website will give you a phone number, and will often give you the name of the person in charge of human resources, or of the sector of the company you are interested in learning about. Do a search.
- The newspaper is an often-overlooked resource. Pay attention to articles on employers who look like they might be expanding. Look up their numbers and give them a call. A good way to start the conversation is to say you saw the piece in the paper.

So, what should I say?

When you're cold calling, the best approach is to take some time and decide what you want to say before you call. Remember, what you want is information. Don't put the employer on the spot by asking them for a job right away. But if the conversation goes well, don't be afraid to politely ask if, or when, there will be any openings.

Write down what you want to say, and some questions to ask. This is especially helpful if you get the person's voice mail. Remember to . . .

- speak clearly
- be very polite
- if someone referred you to that person, start off the conversation by telling them who gave you their name
- ask if you could have a few minutes of their time
- give your name and why you are calling first
- be prepared to talk about your interests and skills
- if the call goes well, ask if there are any suitable positions available either now or in the future.

Here are some examples of things to say to start things off:

- "Hi, my name is _____ _____ . I'm in my last semester as a student at Eastside High, and now I'm looking for a full-time position so I'm gathering some information for my job search. I wonder if you could help me out for a few moments?"
- "Good morning, Mr. Smith. My name is _____ _____ . I'm currently job searching and I'm researching companies in the _____ sector. I was looking at your website yesterday and I had a few questions about your company. I wonder if you have a few minutes to give me some more information?"
- "Hi, it's _____ _____ calling. Jim Lobe suggested I give you a call. I'm gathering some information because I'm job searching at the moment and Jim thought you'd

be a good person to talk to. You see, I'm very interested in companies like yours because _____ ."

TIP Smile on the phone. It will affect how you are heard. And be enthusiastic — it's infectious. People do like helping other people, so give them every reason to think that if they help you, you'll make them feel good by thanking them. Who knows, they might need a favour from you one day.

If you are seriously looking for a job, and not just gathering information for your job search, don't be afraid to come right out and ask the employer if there are any positions available. If the conversation seems to be going well, say something like:

- "I was wondering if you expect to be doing any hiring soon?"
- "May I send along my résumé for you to keep on file in case any positions come up in the near future?"

Remember, if you don't ask, you'll never know. The worst they can say is: "No, not at the moment" or "I'm not sure, I'd have to ask around." So, there is nothing to be afraid of. They might say: "As a matter of fact, we do have an opening coming up soon. Why don't you send me your résumé?"

DOs AND DON'Ts OF JOB SEARCHING

DOs

✓ Do tell everyone you know that you are job searching. Develop a network.

✓ Do look through the newspaper classified ads in the morning. Sometimes jobs fill quickly and the afternoon might be too late.

✓ Do take an application home and fill it out neatly and carefully.

✓ Do dress neatly when you go to job fairs and drop off résumés.

✓ Do be enthusiastic when you are cold calling.

DON'Ts

✗ Don't go unprepared to an information interview. Take the time to learn about the company and prepare some questions.

✗ Don't wait until you move. Look for a job on the Internet before you get there.

✗ Don't feel you have to accept a job if you sense that it's a scam.

✗ Don't ever pay an employer your own money before you start a job.

Where to get more job-searching help . . .

Knowing how and where to look for a job can be difficult when you're starting out. Almost everyone, at some time in their life, has been where you are and knows how difficult it can be. Ask around for some advice. Try a teacher, guidance counsellor, family member, or youth worker. Also, keep in mind that there are professionals at youth employment centres who can help you look for work. Many of these places also list actual jobs and most services are completely free. Check out Chapter 17 for help in finding a centre near you.

7

Before an Interview

"How do I prepare for an interview?"

Always keep a positive attitude when you're job searching. You should be prepared to get a call from an employer asking you in for an interview at any time. It's a good idea to keep your résumé, paper, and a pen beside the phone at all times. That way you'll be ready when the phone rings.

Because it's likely that you'll be applying for several jobs at once, be prepared to respond. When you get a call, don't say, "Which one was that again?" Know the jobs you've applied for. Keep a list by the phone.

Make sure you check your messages frequently if you are out. If an employer calls, return the call as soon as you can. But remember to take a few moments to decide what you're going to say. Have your résumé, pen, and paper handy.

TIP Make sure you have a working answering machine or voice mail on your phone in case you're not home when an employer calls. Tell the people you live with how important it is that you get detailed messages.

What will an employer say when they call me in for an interview?

Here is what the conversation might sound like when an employer calls a young job searcher to set up an interview:

— "Hi, it's John Smith from Noble Company. I've read your résumé and cover letter and I'm calling to find out if you're still interested in applying for the position."

— "Yes, very much."

— "Great. Then I'd like to set up a time for you to come in for an interview. Do you have a pen and paper?"

— "Yes, I do."

— "Okay, we're doing the interviews at the end of the week. How does Friday morning at 10:30 sound?"

— "That's fine for me."

— "Do you know where we are located?"

— "Yes, I know the address, but what's the fastest way there by bus?"

— "Take the number 4 bus from downtown. It comes right past the front door."

— "Thanks. May I take down your phone number and extension in case I need to reach you?"

— "Yes, it's 555-5555, extension 234."

— "Got it, great. Okay, Mr. Smith, I'll see you on Friday morning at 10:30. I'm glad you called and I'm looking forward to meeting you."

TIP Confirm the time and day of the interview at the end of the conversation, just to be sure you've heard correctly, and finish the call with a firm "thank you."

What else should I ask when an employer calls?

In the example above, the candidate asked for clear directions. If you've never been to the place in person, this is a very good question. It'll give you a chance to learn exactly where the company is located and how long it'll take you to get there for your interview. If you honestly don't know the answers, here are some other good questions to ask when an employer calls you in for an interview:

- "Can you confirm the address for me?"
- "Do you have a website I could look at to learn more about the company before the interview?"
- "May I stop by your office and pick up some information on your organization before the interview?"

The employer is listening carefully to how you conduct yourself from the very beginning. Try to be as polite, eager, and confident as you can, even on the first call. It is their first impression of you and you want to make it a good one.

TIP This first conversation, when an employer calls to ask you in for an interview, is not the time ask, "What does the job pay?" The employer will bring up salary or wages if you have a successful interview.

How do I research the company or organization?

It is a very good strategy to research the company or organization to prepare for your interview. Check out the company's website and read all the company history, goals, objectives, mission statements, and frequently asked questions (FAQs). Go to the company and ask the receptionist for their annual report or other company literature. Go to the library and learn more about the industry in general. Search the library for newspaper articles and business directories. Network with people in the same industry to learn more about the company.

If the company manufactures a product, try to find out what it does and where it's sold. If they deliver a service, find out who are their typical clients and who benefits from their service. If you have an interview for a job in a restaurant, try to eat there so you know what's on the menu and the kind of place it is. If you can't make it in to the restaurant before your interview, check to see if they have a website with an online menu. If the job is in a shop, think about the kind of things they sell and the kind of customers they will usually get. The more you know going into an interview, the better you will look to an employer and the more confident you will feel.

How do I research the position?

Some positions are common to many organizations and they will be fairly similar wherever you work. If you've never held a similar position before, then it is important to learn as much about the type of job and its duties as you can. If you know anyone who does a similar job, ask them about it. What do they do in a typical day? What tasks are most important to their employer? This will give you a sense of the kind of skills the employer will be looking for in the interview and you will be better prepared to highlight your own skills in those areas.

TIP Get to the interview a little early and ask if there is any information on the company for you to read.

What should I do the night before an interview?

You might be a little nervous the night before the interview, but it's important to get a good night's sleep. You'll want to be fresh and wide awake during the interview.

If your interview is in the morning, make sure you set your alarm clock. It is very important that you are not late for an interview, as it makes a very poor first impression.

What should I wear to an interview?

Dress nicely. A good rule of thumb is to imagine that you got the job, and picture what you would wear on a typical day. Then, for the interview, dress a little more formally than you would if you

were at work there. Job interviews call for your smartest-looking clothes.

Make sure your clothes are clean, and pressed if they require it. If you feel you don't have the right clothes, try to borrow them for the interview. Ask a friend who is the same size as you. Don't worry about overdressing; they are expecting you to try and impress them. And remember, all the other candidates will be well dressed.

Also, make sure you are clean and well groomed. The effort you put in to looking your best will always be to your advantage.

What should I bring with me to the interview?
Here is a list of things you should bring with you to the interview:

- the exact address, including: suite number, floor, office number, wing, or any other specific directions you were given.
- the name of the person who will be interviewing you.
- the phone number of the company and the extension of the person you're meeting so you can call them in the unlikely event you are running late.
- a separate list of references, typed neatly on a separate sheet. This is important, even if you've already given them to the employer on an application form. A separate sheet shows you are organized and are thinking ahead.

- two extra clean copies of your résumé — one for you to look at during the interview and an extra one for the employer, just in case they've misplaced theirs or they only have a blurry faxed copy.
- three possible prepared questions for the end of the interview (see page 93 for help).
- a notepad or paper, so that you can take notes. Always ask permission to take notes in an interview.

What are references?

A reference is someone who agrees to speak to a potential employer about you and your abilities in a positive way. See pages 13–16 in Chapter 2 for more information about how to choose your references, and what to ask them.

Don't wait until the last minute to get together your references. Be prepared as early as possible and always ask them for permission first.

Should I practise my interview skills?

Yes. Ask someone you trust to help you with your interview skills. Ask them to interview you as a "rehearsal."

Think success and it will happen . . .

During the interview you are likely going to be in a room, sitting in a chair, talking with an employer (or two) across a desk. Imagine yourself sitting up straight, head held high, answering the questions confidently. You should be able to talk easily about what you've done in the past and what you enjoy.

TIP It's okay if you're nervous. If you forget what you were going to say, admit you are nervous and move on. Being nervous is normal. It happens to everyone.

THREE THINGS TO KEEP IN MIND

1. Know what's on your résumé.
2. Answer every question in full. Say more than "Yes" or "No." Give an example from a previous job, hobby, or school experience that illustrates your answer.
3. Sell yourself. Be confident. You will get the job.

What are some common topics I will be asked about?

Be prepared to answer questions related to these topics:

- your previous work experience
- your skills and qualifications
- your preferred work environment
- your education
- your attitude toward the position you're applying for
- your extra-curricular interests, hobbies, and values
- why you want the job
- your availability

What are some tricky questions I can prepare for?

Q: What are your expectations of this job? Why do you want the job?

For a question like this state how you want to do a great job, learn a lot, and make a good contribution to the company.

Q: What did you not like about your previous job?

First, try to say that this is a tough question because you did like your last job. Be specific and state something that you were very successful at, or had a good influence on. Then, pick something you honestly felt wasn't great at your last job, but don't dwell on it. Move on quickly.

Never, never, never say bad things about your previous employer, even if you left on bad terms and you feel you were completely in the right. Employers almost always respond badly to this because they identify with the employer. Make sure you have thought of at least one good thing to say about your previous position. You can't lie about the reason you left a previous job, especially if you were fired, but you can say you've learned a great deal from the experience you had at your last job and would be able to bring that knowledge to this new position.

Q: How long do you intend to be with the company?

If you are applying for a part-time or full-time position, then try not to commit yourself to a specific amount of time. You can simply say that you look forward to being a part of the team and growing with the job. If they press you for an answer it's better to say a longer period of time than a shorter period. Two years is generally appropriate because employers don't like fast turnover, as it takes time to train new people.

Q: Tell me about yourself.

Because this is such a broad request, some people don't know what to say. Give a general overview of education, work experience, and where you're at now. Keep your comments work-related. Stay focused. Be brief. This question is often used to see how well someone can focus and organize their thoughts. Don't ramble on about your childhood.

Q: Where do you see yourself in five years?

This is a good time to be honest. If you've got a long-term goal to go back to school or to do something that you've always dreamed of, then say it. Five years is a long way off, especially for a young person. Showing an employer that you've got dreams and goals is very important. Make sure, however, that your goals sound sufficiently far off that the employer doesn't think you'll want to leave too soon to pursue them. Try to cast the job as a step to realizing your dreams. Perhaps it's an important learning experience for you, or a great way to earn and save some money.

If you are trying to break into a specific field, and the job you're applying for is a career move, then this question is a great opportunity for you to really tell an employer about your goals. Don't be unrealistic or aggressive, just be honest and enthusiastic.

Q: Tell me something about yourself that you want to change. (Or, What is your greatest weakness?)

This is possibly the most common tricky question. The way around it is to come up with a negative quality that is not directly related to the job you're applying for, or to admit to a weakness that you're actively improving. *Whatever you do, have an answer prepared just in case you're asked this question.* After all, everyone has weaknesses and it doesn't look good if you think you have none. Even if you acknowledge that it's a tough question, it's always best to answer rather than not.

There are still good and bad answers to this question. For example, it's better to admit to being "a little competitive at times," or to say, "My best friend says I can be opinionated," than it is to say, "I have trouble getting out of bed in the morning" or "I didn't get along with my last boss." Try to decide on something that's right for you. Make sure you let the employer know how you're taking steps to change the behaviour.

TIP Talk yourself up. Always speak enthusiastically about your experiences. If you have to mention something negative, try to see the good in it. Talk about what you've learned. Give negative experiences a "positive spin." Don't be embarrassed to talk about yourself in a positive light. You don't have to brag — just be confident and only talk about your strengths. An interview is not a time to be shy!

What questions should I ask an employer at the end of an interview?

Many interviews conclude with the employer saying something like this: "I think that's it from me. Do you have any questions?"

Be prepared for this. Take time before the interview to prepare a list of questions. Get out your sheet and take a moment to read them over. Make sure the employer has covered everything on your list. Often, most things will have been covered but it's important to make sure you've learned everything you can about the position.

Even if everything seems to have been covered, it's still good to ask a question or two. Here is a list of some good questions for the end of an interview:

- "If I'm successful, what kind of training would I receive?"
- "Could you tell me the next step in the hiring process?"
- "If I'm successful, who would I report to?"
- "When would the position start?"

CHECKLIST — BEFORE THE INTERVIEW

Make sure you have . . .

- a short list of questions to ask the employer
- two fresh copies of your résumé
- a separate sheet with your references' names, addresses, phone numbers, titles, and relationship to you, typed neatly and in full (see pages 13–16 for more information on references)
- your interview clothes laid out and shoes cleaned
- the directions to the interview, a ride there or bus fare, and an understanding of how long it will take
- the company's phone number, in case you get lost or held up.

DOs AND DON'Ts OF INTERVIEW PREPARATION

DOs

✓ Do treat the initial phone call as the first stage of the interview.

✓ Do be on time.

✓ Do bring copies of your résumé.

✓ Do bring a typed list of references.

✓ Do smile.

✓ Do be polite.

✓ Do give examples.

✓ Do bring the address, phone number, and name of the person interviewing you, so you can call just in case you get lost or delayed.

✓ Do be enthusiastic and have a positive attitude.

✓ Do make eye contact and shake the interviewer's hand firmly.

✓ Do dress nicely — a little better than the job itself would require.

✓ Do thank the interviewer for their time.

✓ Do ask what the next step will be after the interview.

✓ Do give examples of accomplishments.

DON'Ts

✗ Don't lie.

✗ Don't talk too much but don't give one-word answers either.

✗ Don't talk negatively about previous employers.

✗ Don't chew gum.

✗ Don't smoke right before going in — it will smell and might give a bad impression.

✗ Don't be rude to anyone you meet on your way in.

✗ Don't slouch in your seat.

✗ Don't fidget with pen, hair, etc.

I still need more help to prepare for my interview . . .

Interviews can sometimes be difficult to prepare for, especially if it's your first time. Lots of people can help you. Just remember, among your parents, teachers, friends, and siblings you will be able to find someone who has either been through or given an interview at some point in their lives. Ask them to give you a hand. Also, there are lots of places to go to get interview help from professionals. Most services for youth are free. Check out Chapter 17 for help in finding a centre near you.

All About Interviews

"What do I need to know?"

Now we know that the most important part of having a successful interview is to be prepared. Next you are going to find out about the different kinds of interviews, what to expect during the interview, and what to do after it's all over.

What is the employer looking for?

The employer is looking for the right person for the job, and you want them to believe that it's you! So think of an interview as a conversation. You're not in the witness box. Ask questions, respond, relax a little, and *be yourself*. Above all else, SMILE.

Smiling is the best thing you can do for yourself. Remember, this employer is looking to hire someone. That means they will be seeing the person every working day. They do not want to be around someone who is grumpy. A smile means confidence and happiness, and it is always a welcoming sign. It's hard to dislike someone who is smiling.

IMAGINING SUCCESS

As an exercise, picture this scenario: You will be a few minutes early as you walk into the place, approach the first employee you see, and confidently say, "Hi, I'm here to see _____ _____." And they will tell you to have a seat while they let the person know you've arrived. Then you will introduce yourself to the person doing the interview. You'll smile and say your name. In all likelihood they will lead you to a private office or room and you will have a seat and the interview will begin. You are doing great, answering the questions with good examples from your previous experience, and your head is held high. You're even smiling. Toward the end you ask a few good, well-thought-out questions. The interview concludes and you stand up and shake the person's hand, thanking them for their time. You were great. Congratulations.

I'm really nervous, is that normal?

Being nervous is natural. Interviews are almost always a little intimidating for people. Don't lose your cool. If you find yourself feeling nervous, take a few deep breaths. Picture yourself after the interview is all over; feel how good it is to have done a great job in there.

Even if you've never had a job before, or you've only had a little work experience, you can still perform well in an interview. The employer thought enough of you to interview you in the first place! So, you have nothing to lose — just stay focused on the questions. You've done lots of different things in your life, so make sure you're ready to talk about them before you go in to the interview. Answer the questions enthusiastically and give examples of when you acted in that way or accomplished a similar task.

What if I'm late?

If you are late for your interview for a good reason, like the bus you were on had an accident, or there was a traffic jam due to bad weather, then tell the employer right away. Say something like:

- "I'm extremely sorry I'm late, but there was an accident . . ."

Don't dwell on it. Apologize and move on. But do give yourself lots of time to get to the interview. It's better to be really early and sit in a nearby coffee shop for half an hour than it is to be late.

If something happens at the last minute and you can't make the interview, but you still really want the job, call the employer. Tell them an emergency has come up and ask if you could possibly re-schedule your interview time.

How long do interviews last?

Some interviews last only a few minutes, while others last more than an hour. It all depends on the person, the job, and what has to be accomplished in the interview. As a general rule, most interviews are between 20 and 40 minutes long.

Are all interviews the same?

No, although most are pretty similar. A standard interview is a face-to-face meeting between an employer and a candidate in a private office or area. They take the form of a discussion based on questions posed by the employer and answers given by the candidate. But sometimes employers do conduct different types of interviews. Here are a few other kinds:

Telephone Interview

One-on-one Interview

Panel Interview

Group Interview

Written interviews

Some job interviews have a written part that is conducted either before or after a normal face-to-face interview. Often the written part is an aptitude or personality-type test made up of multiple-choice questions. Some employers use these tests to help them decide who to hire. It gives them one more way to assess a candidate. Take these tests seriously and do your best. Employers who use them do so because they feel they are important.

Telephone interviews

Some organizations give interviews over the phone. Usually a phone interview means there will be more than one round of interviews. If you do well on a phone interview, it will likely be followed by a second, in-person interview.

If the phone interview is going to involve more than a few simple screening questions, then the employer will likely call you first and set up a time to call you back. This will give you time to prepare as though it were a face-to-face interview. Phone interviews can sometimes take just as long as in-person interviews, so take them seriously. Have your résumé and a pen and paper handy during the interview.

Remember, whenever you are talking to an employer on the phone, treat the conversation as an interview because you want the employer to form a good opinion of you. It may even help you to actually dress up a bit for phone interviews. Many people say it helps them "feel professional." So change out of your pajamas and put on your good clothes so you'll sound as good as you look!

Group interviews

In some cases there will be more than one candidate in the room at the same time, making the interview seem more competitive. These types of interviews are conducted for many different reasons, but **the good news is** that usually it is because the company or organization is going to be hiring more than one person, and is looking for a "team." By interviewing more than one candidate at a time, the employer can save time interviewing and also see how the successful candidates interact.

Just be yourself. Remember, if you get the job you want to be happy doing it. So act naturally, and if you are successful it should be a good fit for your personality type.

Panel interviews or multiple interviewers

In another common type of interview, more than one person will be interviewing you. There are many different reasons why employers do this. Often, employers have two people conduct the interview when the job requires a candidate who will be supervised by more than one person. Because different people have different perspectives, an employer wants to hire someone that everyone agrees will be suitable for the position.

If you find yourself in this type of interview, direct your answers to the person who asked the question, but make sure to have eye contact with both the interviewers. It is important to impress all the people in the room because when you leave, they will have a discussion based on your performance in the interview.

Behaviour-based interviews

More and more employers use behaviour-based interviews to ask questions about an applicant's accomplishments and skills to see if they match what the employer is looking for. The employer wants to know how you would think and act in certain situations. Behaviour-based questions are specific — you have to provide examples of what you did in different circumstances.

Some behaviour-based questions might include:

- "Tell me about a time you worked as part of a team."
- "Have you ever worked on a team with someone you didn't get along with? How did you handle it?"
- "Tell me about a time when you had to deal with a difficult problem. What was the problem and how did you solve it?"

Take the time to think about your answer. Don't be in a hurry. Employers know that you need time to think about your reply. Be sure to give specific examples of what you have done to demonstrate the skills they're looking for. Emphasize skills such as leadership, problem solving, teamwork, or meeting deadlines.

Sell yourself and be positive. The question may seem negative: "Can you describe a situation where you made a bad decision?" Turn your answer from a negative to a positive. Respond with what you learned from the situation and how you would handle it differently next time.

The truth is, you'll have to be ready for anything when you go into an interview situation. Just do your best and react positively to whatever type of interview an employer uses.

TIP Make a good first impression. Smile. Shake the interviewer's hand firmly and make eye contact, saying, "It's nice to meet you." Don't worry if you're a little nervous. It shows that you want the job and that you are concerned about how the interview will go.

What are some typical interview questions?

For a list of typical topics, see page 90.

What are some especially tricky questions?

For a list of tricky questions and some ways to answer them, see pages 90–92. Make sure you have prepared answers to these questions ahead of time.

When can I ask about "the money"?

It's natural to be curious about what the job pays if the wage or salary is not mentioned in the ad, or you are applying for a job that wasn't advertised. If you are expecting to be paid a wage or salary that is more than minimum wage, it's a good idea to ask about the pay at the end of the interview. If the job does not pay what you were expecting then you will avoid disappointment later. Always be polite and courteous when asking.

The best idea is to try to determine the pay range for the position before you go into an interview. This is especially true if you are applying for a job to support yourself, because you have to know how much you will need to live on. If you're in this situation, make a list of all the things you have to pay for each month and add them up. Make sure the salary for the job covers those expenses. A part-time job probably won't give you enough money if you're on your own. You may need two part-time jobs or one full-time job to make sure you can pay your rent, buy food, and pay the bills. Plus, you are going to want some left over to get other stuff — this is what will make it all worthwhile.

Be realistic with your salary expectations. Many entry-level jobs pay minimum wage or slightly higher. It is illegal for an employer to pay less than the minimum wage. (To find out the minimum wage in your province, call your ministry of labour. Look up the number in the "blue pages" section of your phone book.) Pay rates vary between communities, industries, and sectors. Ask friends who do similar jobs. Make sure the wage for the job you want is right for your situation.

When should I hand over my references?

Some employers insist that you list your references on the application form when you first apply, while others won't ask for them until the end of an interview. Not all employers check references, but most do. That's why it's best to be prepared with your references before you start your job search. Type them on a separate sheet and bring them with you to the interview.

Use only references that will speak positively about you. If you have doubts, don't use them. See pages 13–16 for more information on references.

Second interviews

Sometimes, but not always, employers will call you in for a second interview. The second interview is a chance for an employer to . . .

- talk with the final few candidates one more time
- have another manager conduct the final interview
- ask different questions to help them make their decision.

Second interviews usually mean that the employer has narrowed down the hiring to two or three people. It's your chance to really shine. The employer will expect you to be really prepared. Make sure you've read any information they may have given you after the first interview. You've done very well to get this far. Good job!

How did I do? When will I find out?

One of the last questions you should ask at an interview is: "When do you anticipate making your decision?"

Sometimes an employer will take a few hours, other times a few days, maybe even weeks to make a decision about who to hire. Even if a job interview goes well, don't stop looking. There might be an even better job that comes up in the meantime. Of course it rarely happens, but the best position to be in is to have more than one job offer.

Should I make a follow-up call or write a follow-up letter?

It's up to you, but a very short letter sent by fax or e-mail is an easy way to thank the employer for the interview and re-state your interest in the position. If you decide to call, it might be a good idea to call after business hours and leave a short voice-mail message. In a thank-you message or letter it's generally not advisable to mention things you forgot to say in an interview or get into detail about why they should hire you.

Here is an example of a good follow-up note.

These days many people send a short follow-up letter. It shows that you really

---

Brett Cooper
4 Spruce St., Sudbury, ON P3A 2K4
(705) 555-1818

October 5, 2005
Robert Arnold
Manager, Office Co. Ltd.
4 Regent St.,
Sudbury, ON P3E 4A2

Dear Mr. Arnold:

Just a short note to thank you for my interview yesterday. I enjoyed meeting you. I remain very interested in the _____ position and look forward to hearing from you soon.

Sincerely,

Brett Cooper

Brett Cooper

---

want the job and it is a polite way to keep your name alive in a busy employer's mind.

I don't think it's the right job for me

What do you do if over the course of an interview you realize that you don't want the job? Perhaps it involves longer hours than you were expecting, or the location is too difficult or costly to get to, or the wage is far too low, or the job itself is not what you were expecting at all. First of all, because no one wants to turn down a job and regret it later, it's a good idea to talk something like this over with someone you trust. Tell them your concerns, what's bugging you about it. Try to make a firm decision about whether or not you want the job. Perhaps you'll take it and give it a try, or take it for now but keep looking for something more suitable. If you do decide to take the job, then great.

If you've decided against it, then it's polite to let the employer know that you are withdrawing your application, because someone else out there probably really wants the job and is waiting to find out. You could call the employer and let them know, or else e-mail or fax them a short note.

I got the job!

Accepting the position is the next big step. When an employer calls to offer you a job you should already have decided what you are going to say. If it's yes, then congratulations. But in the excitement, don't forget to clarify a few things before you accept:

- What does the job pay?
- When do you start?
- Who do you report to on the first day?
- How long are the workdays or shifts?
- What is your schedule for the first week?
- Is there a dress code or uniform?

I didn't get the job . . .

If you had an interview but didn't get the job, an employer will sometimes call and let you know. Other times, they will send you a letter. They won't say very much, and probably won't really tell you why — even if you ask — so if they call, just keep the conversation short.

The important thing is to not lose heart. It happens to everyone many times over the course of a lifetime. Why people choose one person over another is sometimes hard to understand. It's okay and really normal to be disappointed, but move on quickly. Don't let it get to you. Just the fact that you got an interview means there is something special about you. If one employer thought so, others will too. Getting an interview is a success in itself. There are many great jobs out there for you. So what are you waiting for?

DOs AND DON'Ts OF INTERVIEWS

DOs

✓ Do make a good first impression.

✓ Do smile.

✓ Do imagine success.

✓ Do be ready to face any type of interview.

✓ Do bring along two fresh copies of your résumé and your reference sheet. Do research the position and find out the salary range before you apply.

DON'Ts

✗ Don't ask about "the money" until the end of the interview.

Where to get more help for your interview

Knowing how to be successful in an interview can be difficult when you're starting out. Almost everyone has been where you are at some point and knows how difficult it can be. Ask a teacher, guidance counsellor, family member, or youth worker for advice, or seek out professionals at youth employment centres who can help you work on your interview skills. Check out Chapter 17 for help in finding a centre near you.

9

Success on the Job

"How will I know what to do?"

Congratulations on your new job! Let's take a look at what you should know and what you can expect from your new job. You want to do a great job for many reasons, like . . .

- you don't want to have to look for another one soon!
- you want to work to make the money you need
- you want to do well so when it's time to get another job, you'll have good references, you'll have learned a lot, and you'll have gained experience.

I'm nervous about my first day . . .

Everyone gets nervous about their first day. Just make sure you . . .

- set your alarm clock
- get up on time
- leave early, giving yourself lots of time to get there ten minutes before you are supposed to start
- bring something to eat, or some money to buy food if there is somewhere nearby to do so
- choose what you want to wear the night before

- know exactly how to get to your new job
- know who you are reporting to.

What can I expect on my first day on the job?

Your new boss will expect you to be there on time and ready to start. You will probably have training on the first day. Sometimes this means you will learn from the person who was in the position before you, or another staff member — or even the boss — may be in charge of training you.

You won't be expected to learn it all in one day, but be eager to learn all that the job requires. Depending on what the job is, it'll take some time to get good at it. Pay attention to everything you are told, and don't be afraid to ask questions. At the beginning it's better to ask a lot of questions than to do a task incorrectly and have to re-do it. Taking notes can be very helpful if it's the sort of job where there are lots of details to remember.

TIP Be ready for anything and be flexible. It may be hard to remember everything, but you will learn it all in time.

You will also meet new people. At the beginning, you probably won't be able to remember everyone's name, their roles, and how they might affect you and your job. Remember, everyone had a first day once too. Co-workers are going to ask you about yourself, so be prepared to smile and say a few words about where you've come from or what you've been doing up to this point. People are always curious about someone new. You'll be spending a lot of time with these people, so be friendly without talking too much. It's best to save your long conversations for the breaks, lunch, or after work.

What should I wear?

When you went to your interview, did you get a chance to see what other people were wearing? Was there a dress code or a uniform? If so, your employer probably told you about it when you were offered the job. If not, then dress as nicely as you can and be prepared to find out more on your first day. Remember, you're not expected to know it all from day one, so just dress neatly and comfortably. You'll feel a lot better about it tomorrow when you know more about what's expected of you.

Do I get a break?

Yes, of course you get a break. But people are often busy at work and may forget to tell you about it. So during your training on the first day, make sure you remember to ask your boss or a co-worker when the breaks are and whether or not you are paid for that time. These aren't dumb questions, since breaks differ from workplace to workplace. Don't let the issue slide by because you are too shy to ask.

Make sure you return from your break on time. Your boss and co-workers depend on you to be punctual.

TIP An employer must give you a break to eat, even if you are working a part-time shift. If you find you're not getting breaks, ask your supervisor about the best time to take your breaks. If the response is not satisfactory, call your local ministry of labour (look in the "blue pages" of your phone book) and find out your rights when it comes to breaks. It is very important that you be allowed to stop work and take a break, eat, and use the washroom.

What if I've never done this task before?

Every new job will involve some tasks that you've never done before. Just be honest and tell the person training you that this is new to you. Ask them to show you how it's done first. Don't guess. You'll pick it up. Never be afraid to ask for help. Be as flexible in the beginning as you can.

When do I get paid?

Every company and organization has a different pay schedule. Most pay bi-weekly, which means one paycheque every two weeks (for example, a cheque every second Friday). Others pay semi-monthly, which means two paycheques per month (for example, a cheque on the first of the month and another on the fifteenth). Ask about when your first paycheque will arrive. It's important to be prepared and to make sure you can make your money last.

These days, many companies can pay you by direct deposit. This means they will electronically deposit your money directly into your bank account. To do this you will need to open a bank account and give them a blank cheque with the word "VOID" written across it, or they will need your savings account number and your branch number. This is the fastest and easiest way to get your paycheque. Your employer will still give you a paper record of the deposit as proof that you've been paid.

Other companies prefer to give you an actual cheque for you to deposit. Make sure you check with your bank to see if there is a holding period on cheques deposited in your account by an ATM. If there is you might have to wait a week before you can get at your money. Talk to your bank and they will tell you your options regarding depositing cheques.

If you have questions about taxes and deductions, see pages 114–15 for more information.

TIP One thing you can do after a little while is ask to see the company's human resources policies and procedures information (sometimes called a "procedures manual") — if they haven't already given it to you to read. Not every workplace will have a policy manual, especially if the company is small, but many do. In the manual you will find the company's rules concerning sick days, leave, benefits, pay days, harassment complaint procedures, dress code rules, vacation time, and many other rules and regulations the company has set out for its employees.

A company's HUMAN RESOURCES or PERSONNEL department is in charge of policies and procedures concerning the employees in the company. It often takes care of things like hiring staff, booking vacation time, payroll, sick days, leaves of absence, firing, and benefits packages. It is a good place to go if you need information or have a question or concern.

What are "commission" and "base pay"?

If you are working at a job that involves selling, you will probably need to know about commission. Commission pay is based on what, and how much, you sell. Usually sales jobs also have a "base pay." Base pay is an hourly wage that you earn no matter how much you sell, and the commission is the money you make on top of this. Many great sales jobs have some commission or "bonus pay" attached to them to give you incentive to work hard, sell lots, and do a good job.

When is commission not a good idea?

Some people are very good at sales and they make a lot of money, but they know how to do it and have a lot of experience. If you've never sold before, be careful of 100% commission jobs. You might work a whole week, not sell anything, and therefore not get paid. Accept that selling is hard if you've never done it before, and that at the beginning you will probably not make the thousands of dollars a week that they say you can. It may take time to get that good at it. If you want a sales job, start by taking one that has base pay plus commission, just to be safe, and make sure you understand and agree to how the pay system works before you start.

I didn't realize what sales involved . . .

Sometimes young people take sales jobs, only to find that they aren't good at it or don't like it. Often this is because jobs that involve direct selling, either over the phone or door to door, pay by commission only. The uncertainty this causes about how much they will get paid is sometimes too risky for young people. Other times they don't like the pressure. If you're good at sales then you will know right away and you'll likely do very well. If you find sales isn't for you, then begin a new job search as quickly as possible. It's good to discover what you like and dislike in the working world. It will help you make better decisions in the future.

What if I'm sick or need time off?

If you wake up one morning and find that you're sick and are unable to make it into work, then you must call your boss as soon as he or she arrives at work. Try not to leave voice mail — do your best to talk to them directly and tell them what's wrong with you and why you won't be in. Depending on the province you live in, the kind of job you have, and the company you work for, you may not be paid for sick days. This is especially true at the beginning of your employment period.

Everyone gets sick and has to take the occasional day off work. If it's serious and you are going to need several days off, talk to your boss. You will probably have to get a note from your doctor.

If you need some time off, say a few hours, to go to a doctor's appointment, or to register for school, or for some other important engagement, then make sure you ask your employer well in advance. Most employers realize that things come up, and are happy to work around them. Just don't leave it to the last minute to tell your supervisor. You don't want to leave them understaffed.

Is this job safe?

Never agree to do a task that you feel is dangerous or unsafe. Instead, tell your employer that you feel the task is dangerous. Show them why. Try to work something out. Most employers will never put you in danger on purpose. If you are having a problem in this area, then call the ministry of labour in your province. You can find their number in the "blue pages" section of your phone book.

What are payroll taxes and deductions?

When you started your job, you should have filled out a form that tells the employer how much tax to take off your paycheque. Unless you are a student and you checked off the box saying you will not make the minimum amount this year to have tax deducted, your cheque will have less on it than you might be expecting.

Working out how much tax is being taken off can be a little tricky, and these days it's often done by computer programs, so just ask your employer to explain the various deductions.

In addition to tax, there will also be deductions made for the Canada Pension Plan (CPP), Employment Insurance (EI), and if you're in a union, union dues. Some companies also make other deductions for health plans or, if you've requested it, RRSP contributions. Just ask your boss or the person on payroll to go over your pay stub with you. If there are deductions being made, then they must be listed on your pay stub.

While you are working you are also entitled to earn vacation pay for every hour you work. Depending on your job, some employers pay this on every cheque; others let it build up. Make sure to ask for your vacation pay when you leave.

TIP If you are receiving your wages in cash and there are no tax deductions being made, you might be getting paid illegally. This is often called getting paid "under the table." It is against the law not to pay tax. You also may not be on record as an employee, which might mean you won't have rights if you are hurt at work, or you want to take a vacation, or any of the other things that are provided under the law for people who work in Canada. Talk to your employer and find out if they are making tax deductions. Make sure they are paying you legally. If you have any concerns, talk to your parents, or call the ministry of labour in your province (the number is in the "blue pages" section of your phone book).

It's best not to discuss your salary, wage, or deductions with other staff members or colleagues until you've been there a while. Keep it between you and your boss or supervisor at the beginning. People do not tend to show their pay stubs to other workers because it is private information, and knowing what others get paid can lead to bad feelings. Use your own judgement, but in most cases your salary is a matter for you and your employer to discuss.

What happens if I find myself in a job I think is a scam?

If you find yourself doing a job that makes you very upset or uncomfortable, then it's okay to look for another job. If doing a job makes you act or treat other people in a way that is unfair or misleading, even illegal, then quit.

If you are concerned about a job being "for real," then ask someone you trust, like a parent or teacher or friend, for advice. Tell them you're worried the job is not everything they say it is. Ask them to help you decide what to do. Don't be embarrassed. Don't keep it to yourself.

What is a performance evaluation?

Most employers will have periodic meetings with you to discuss your job performance. Together you will review your performance on the job and discuss any improvements that need to be made. It is a good time to let your boss know about any problems you are having at work, or any expectations you feel are unrealistic. These meetings usually happen after the first three months, then possibly again after six months or a year. (See the section on probation on page 121.)

Getting feedback about your performance on the job helps you to do a better job and improve as you go. It's important to ask, every now and then, "How am I doing?" Feedback is especially important at the beginning of a job. Ask how you are doing, and whether you can do better somehow. Take the criticism in a good way. It will help you do better and succeed.

What are my rights on the job?

As an employee working in Canada your rights are protected under the law. If you are experiencing harassment, unsafe work conditions, unfair pay, mistreatment, discrimination, or abuse on the job, then speak up. Tell someone you trust what is going on at work. Don't keep quiet. You're not alone and it's not your fault. Your employer and colleagues are not allowed to mistreat you at work.

If you don't have anyone to talk to, call your provincial ministry of labour and ask them for advice. You won't have to give your name or tell them the employer's name to get advice. Your rights are protected under the law.

What's a union?

Unions are organizations that look after and protect the interests of workers. If you get a job in a company that has a union, you may be required to become a member. If you do, and you have questions about what role your union plays in your workplace, make sure you ask your union representative whatever is on your mind.

Relationships with co-workers and employers

A good working relationship with your boss, co-workers, and other staff is worth developing right from the start. You'll be spending every workday with these people, so you'll need to get along well together. Start things off on the right foot. When you meet them, take some time to ask them a question or two about what they do at work and what their job entails. Always be polite and courteous.

You may not become great friends with everyone you work with, but that's fine — you're not expected to. What's important is to strike a balance. A good working relationship means that you can work with someone in a way that is friendly, professional, and respectful.

If you find you're having a problem with a co-worker, try talking to them about it. Make sure you pick a good time when it's not too busy at work. Don't yell or get angry. Tell them how you are feeling and why. Don't blame or accuse them. Simply address the specific problem you've been having. Be polite but firm and try to offer a solution. Try asking something like:

- "I don't understand why you got angry with me over _____ ."

- "I would really like to try and work together better. How can I improve things?"

If talking to your co-worker doesn't seem to change anything, or they don't respond in a favourable way, then it's time to take a moment and speak to your boss about the problem.

Try to resolve work problems when they arise. Don't let them sit and get worse.

DOs OF WORKPLACE RELATIONSHIPS

✓ Do be honest and direct in your communication.

✓ Do go first to the person with whom you are having the problem. If you are unsuccessful, then go to your supervisor.

✓ Do try to resolve the issue right away.

✓ Do speak honestly with your supervisor if the problem is with them.

✓ Do listen carefully to the other person's point of view. They may have good reasons for their behaviour.

I'm having a really big problem . . .

Trust your instincts. Occasionally people have bad experiences at work. If you're experiencing discrimination or harassment at work by a co-worker, then speak to your boss immediately. If you can't, or it's your boss who is the problem, talk to someone you trust. Tell them what's happening to you, even if you're not sure it is discrimination or harassment.

Don't keep it a secret or blame yourself. When something is seriously wrong, when someone is not treating you the right way, do something about it. It's just going to get worse if you keep it to yourself.

CHECKLIST — MY SUMMER JOB IS ENDING

If it's almost September and you're going back to school, don't forget the following:

• Ask your employer for a letter of reference (see pages 13–16).

• Ask how you go about getting hired next summer, if that's something you might want.

• Find out if they need part-time or occasional help during the school year. You might need some money near the holidays.

• Make sure you leave your address with the employer in case there is vacation pay or a final paycheque still to come after you're finished.

Should I ask for a letter of reference?

Although most future employers will want to actually speak to your last employer on the phone when they are checking your references, it's always nice insurance to have a written letter of reference. If a company goes out of business, or you lose contact with a former boss because they move or leave the company, a letter is some proof that you did a good job and were a good employee. Letters of reference are also helpful if you move from one city or town to another.

I'm out of here!

People leave jobs for many reasons. If you are thinking of quitting, make sure you give at least two weeks' notice. Depending on the situation, you might think it's polite to give your boss more notice. People understand that everyone has to move on to new jobs, or go back to school, or go travelling at some point, so just make sure you are courteous and give enough notice. You will likely need the employer to be a reference for your next job search, even if it isn't going to be soon.

Many young people work in shops or restaurants where work is done in shifts. One of the risks of giving two weeks' notice in those positions is that people find they get fewer shifts than they'd like in the final two weeks of work. It's up to you how you want to deal with your specific situation, but usually if you treat people with respect and give them fair notice, then they will return the respect. By the time you are ready to leave you will probably know if this is true of your employer.

My contract's ending . . .

Many jobs are called contract positions. This means you agree to work for a specific amount of time, such as several weeks, three months, six months, or a year. Contracts are a great way to get your foot in the door and get full-time work experience. And they may even lead to a permanent position.

But eventually the contract will end, and if there is no way the company or organization can keep you on, it's time for you to start looking for another position. If you're finding it hard to get another job right away and you need money for rent and food, you may be eligible to collect Employment Insurance (EI). To find out if you qualify, call Human Resources Development Canada by looking up "employment insurance" in the "blue pages" of the phone book.

If you know your contract is going to end, try to plan ahead. Now that you've been working, you have a whole new set of contacts. Start your job search before the contract is over. Let everyone you've met in your job know that your contract is unfortunately ending and that you'll be looking for a new position soon. Ask them to let you know if they hear of any openings at other companies.

I've been "let go." What happens now?

There are many reasons why people are "let go." Sometimes companies "lay people off" because they are cutting back on staff. Other times workers are fired.

Whether you've been let go because of cutbacks or because you've been fired, it's an awful feeling if you didn't see it coming. Take some time to reflect on why you were let go and what this means to you. Were you happy in your job? Do you want to change jobs or look for another similar job? You will have many questions. Try to talk about your situation with someone you trust. Make some plans for the future, both short-term and long-term. It's likely to be a difficult time for you now but it will pass, and you will find another position soon. The sooner you begin looking, the better.

If you are being fired after your probation period is over, the employer must tell you why. Make sure it's a legitimate reason. If it's something you did or failed to do, then make sure you get it in writing. Depending on how long you've worked there, it shouldn't be the first time you're hearing about it. If you have questions or concerns about why you were fired, then call your local ministry of labour (their phone number is in the "blue pages" section of the phone book).

PROBATION PERIOD is the period of time at the beginning of a job when you and the employer can decide if you are a good match for the position. Probation periods often last three months, but could be shorter or longer — be sure to find out when yours ends.

TIP If you suspect you are not doing a good job, and you are worried about losing your job, talk to your employer about it. Ask for more training, guidance, and feedback. You may be able to correct the problem before it gets too bad.

One of the main reasons people lose their jobs is because they have poor personal skills to be able to deal with others in the workplace. Communication problems feature in most dismissals. Other common reasons include an inability to do the job, refusal to do a task, theft, breaking a contract, ongoing lateness or being absent or unreliable, and misconduct. Take every step available to you to do a good job. Know what is expected of you. Read your job description carefully, ask questions, and try to exceed the basic requirements.

I think I need more training or qualifications . . .

You will soon find out that training and learning never stop. Just because you might have finished school, or dropped out of school, it doesn't mean that you won't want to upgrade your skills to earn more money or get a better job. Many employers encourage their staff to take night school, community college courses, or even university courses to gain more knowledge if it will help them on the job. They will often pay for some of it too. Ask your boss or the person in charge of human resources in your company if the company is willing to pay for some or all of a course you'd like to take.

One thing to consider is that if the employer does pay, you may have to agree to stay with the company for a certain amount of time following the course. Is this what you want? If so, then great. If you want to go back to school to upgrade your skills so you can get a better job somewhere else, then it's best to try to pay for it yourself. An employer will be unlikely to give you a good reference if they pay for your courses and then you take your new skills somewhere else.

I'd like to go back to school full-time

It's always a good idea to return to school if you didn't finish high school or would like to do some post-secondary courses. School diplomas give you access to better jobs later — jobs that pay more, jobs that will give you opportunity for promotion, jobs that are more interesting to go to every day. School *now* is a great way to get what you want *later* in life. Stay in it for as long as you can.

10

Deciding to Start a Business

"I don't want a job . . . do I want a business?"

NEW TOY COMING TO STORES

Do I want to be my own boss?

Many young people start out in the workforce wondering why they don't fit in, don't enjoy what they're doing, or can't stay at a job for any length of time. They are full of creative ideas, but are unsure how to use those ideas to make money. Some innovative young people, like Robin, an artist and toy-maker, use their talents to start their own businesses.

TRUE STORY

Robin held many different jobs, but never felt appreciated for all of her hard work. She would work very hard at a job, but after a while, when she found her work wasn't appreciated, she would stop caring about the quality of work she was doing, quit, and move on to the next job.

"I went to school for art . . . and got jobs in various art fields, but I was never doing exactly what I wanted," says Robin. "It was never challenging or creative enough, or the effort required to get somewhere in a field wasn't worth the reward of getting there."

Robin comes from a family of entrepreneurs. Her mother, father, and brother started their own businesses, so it was natural for her to make the decision to become an entrepreneur. She still works for someone else part-time to pay her bills while she works full-time on her business, but she says: "I can't imagine spending my life working hard and not having fun in my jobs, and quitting them as I inevitably feel undervalued."

Self-employment isn't for everyone. Starting a business takes a lot of hard work, dedication, and discipline to be your own boss. The next section of this book deals with the major issues you need to know when considering starting your own business. Take the quiz that follows, then read on to find out if you have what it takes to become an entrepreneur.

- Are you currently in a job but think about starting your own business all the time?
- Do you say, "I just know I want to work for myself?"
- Are you passionate about starting a new product or service?

You might be a typical young entrepreneur . . . cut out to be self-employed. That's reason to celebrate and feel good about yourself.

Lots of people get great satisfaction in their work. They work for others but enjoy what they do. You may be the kind of person who needs and wants to work for themselves. The security of a weekly paycheque is not that important. You want a challenge, work best on your own, or see yourself running your own successful business.

Whatever the case, believe in yourself and get started. The next chapters will walk you through the most important steps to starting a business.

Open my own company?

Starting your own business guarantees you the freedom to work on your own terms. It also gives you the opportunity to set and attain your own goals. No one tells you what to do, because you are the boss. You might have discovered a niche (a special area of demand for a product or service) for your cool product or for one of your skills.

All of your hard work and long hours directly benefit you, rather than increasing someone else's profits. And who doesn't hope that a brilliant idea will earn them piles of money? You make money selling a product or service you're passionate about. And you're always learning and facing new challenges.

Are you ready to start your own business?

Not everyone is cut out to start a business — even people who have great ideas and know how to make them into products or services they can sell don't always have what it takes to work for themselves. Below is a self-assessment quiz to help you decide if starting your own business is a good idea for you. On a piece of scrap paper, write "yes" for each statement you agree with, and "no" for each one you disagree with. Be honest.

SELF-EMPLOYMENT ASSESSMENT QUIZ

1. I want to control how much money I make, so that if I work harder, I can make more money.
2. I don't like working for other people. I like being my own boss, and answering only to myself and my customers.
3. I want to be in control of when I work. I don't mind working long hours, day and night, if it's my choice to do so.
4. I am good at making decisions.
5. I want to create things.
6. I can predict a trend before it happens.
7. I'm the type of person who always finds or creates opportunities.
8. When I have a good idea, I do something about it.

9. When an opportunity comes my way, I grab it.

10. I'm not afraid of change. In fact I look forward to it.

11. I'm always looking for ways to improve things.

12. I have a skill, a product, or a service that somebody would want to pay for.

13. I've worked in a business like the one I want to start.

14. I have some experience in the industry I'm interested in.

15. I already have a contract for some work, and I know some other people who might become clients — possibly enough potential clients to keep my business afloat for the first year.

16. I have trustworthy contacts in the legal and accounting professions who can help me set up my business.

17. I enjoy chasing contracts and making sales, meeting people and finding out how I can help them.

18. I have savings or someone to financially support me or I'm willing to work a part-time job through the rough spots, during the first six months or so of my new business.

19. My family is very supportive of my business plans.

20. I'm generally healthy.

21. I'm generally pretty strong emotionally — when things get rough, I don't get too down or lose my enthusiasm and drive.

22. I don't mind giving up hours of my personal time and sacrificing my personal life to my business.

23. I like working alone, most of the time.

24. I'm pretty self-reliant. I don't need other people to set my priorities or solve my problems.

25. I'm organized enough to manage my tasks and my time.

26. I'm disciplined and I finish what I start.

27. I believe that customers are usually right, and I'm willing to adapt the way I work in order to keep a customer.

28. I believe in the saying: "You have to spend money to make money."

If you agreed with most of these statements, and the rest make some sense to you, then there's a good chance that you have what it takes to go into business for yourself.

Starting a business takes more than having a great idea and being willing to put your energy and time behind it.

WHAT IS A . . .

freelancer? An independent worker, not on salary, hired on a per-project basis.

entrepreneur? Someone who starts and manages a business.

self-employed person? Someone who works for profit in their own business, profession, or trade, or operates a farm.

small business? An independently owned and operated business that usually has fewer than 100 employees.

micro business? A very small business, usually home-based, with fewer than five employees that needs less than $35,000 to get started.

"I always knew what I wanted, and one of those was my own business so I just read up on how to get started and did it."

— Jason, 23, young entrepreneur

I'm young; can I succeed in business?

Being young doesn't mean that you're unable to start a business. You might have a few more challenges than an older person who has more savings or experience behind them, but that shouldn't discourage you from following your dream.

Why am I more likely to succeed?

Some of the qualities that young people tend to have that make them good entrepreneurs include:

- Confidence. Your confidence will help you get where you're going. When you're confident, others can feel it and want to believe in what you have to say, and also want to help you get there.
- Energy. Life hasn't had a chance to wear you down. You can easily take on new challenges without becoming

exhausted. This will come in handy when you need to work 60 hours a week while trying to get your business off the ground.

- Optimism. A positive outlook will help you get through the ups and downs of starting a new business.
- Low expenses. Even if you don't still live at home, you probably aren't carrying a lot of expenses like a mortgage or a high debt-load. Having low living expenses means that you can take more financial risks and funnel your earnings into your business.
- Supportive family and friends. Your family and friends want you to be happy, and they will help you to succeed. They may even help you find customers or refer you to other people.

Youth and energy are clear advantages to starting a business — but it's up to you to demonstrate this to the people who can help you.

Where can I get more information?

The next section of this book has a lot of information to help you get started, so start right here. However, there are lots of resources beyond what is covered in this book. Start with Chapter 17, where there are a lot of websites listed. If you know anyone who has started a business, ask them questions. Look into entrepreneurial programs through community centres or agencies.

11

I Have a Great Idea ... What Next?

"Everyone's going to love this!"

You've decided that you really want to start a business. You have the energy, you're committed to the goal. What's more, you've come up with a great idea. Maybe you have a talent or a skill that you think you could make money from. You might be working in an industry and think you could do better selling your skills for yourself. Or, you're not sure if starting your own business is the right way to go, and you'd like to know more about what's involved. This chapter outlines what you need to know before you get started on your business.

Can I make money from my skills?

Some skills and interests translate into a business more easily than others. Your first step is research. Make sure you understand the industry you're interested in, and the people who will buy your product or service. Read trade magazines and newspapers, and go to the library to find out about the industry.

Use the Internet to research what other products or services are out there, and if your company will have competition, locally or worldwide. Is there another company in your area that offers the product or service you want to offer? If someone else offers a similar product or service, find out what they're doing, how they're doing it, if you would be selling to the same people, and if there's room for another similar product or service on the market.

Check out the competition. Seeing what the competition does and how they do it will help you figure out what makes your company different. If the competition offers a good product but they lack customer service skills, then make a quality product *and* offer good customer service. If your house-sitting service includes a special feature, such as taking care of animals for a small fee, then focus on that selling feature when telling people about your new business.

WHAT SHOULD I CALL MY BUSINESS?

You need to find a name that is suitable for the market you're competing in. It should be short and memorable, and distinctive enough to separate you from your competitors. Make sure it doesn't copy an existing business name. Register your domain name, even if you aren't ready to use it yet, to make sure you get the name you want when you build your website.

TIP Go to one of the Domain Registrar companies on the web. Search for the name first, and if it isn't already being used then apply to the same company for your name, pay the fee, and you have your own domain name for your website.

Why do businesses fail?

Many small businesses fail within the first three years of starting up. Often an entrepreneur has great ideas but just doesn't have the skills or support to make a business work. Somebody can create a great product, but be so disorganized that he or she never gets invoices or bills sent or fails to promote the service. If you know the risks you face, and you understand the difficulties in creating a business, you can plan to overcome those difficulties.

So what do other entrepreneurs do wrong?

- *Fail to realistically self-evaluate*
  You need to be aware of and honest about your strengths, weaknesses, needs, and desires. Ask your support network — your family, friends, and business partners — for honest, objective feedback and criticism, and listen to what they tell you.
- *Fail to set goals*
  You need to have clear, specific, and realistic goals for your business, both for the long-term and for each day, week, and month. Prepare a business plan that outlines your goals.
- *Fail to revise goals*
  Over time, as you learn more and as your situation changes, you need to re-examine your goals to make sure you can still achieve them and that they're still the right goals for you.
- *Fail to avoid obstacles*
  It's important to stay positive, but too much optimism can seriously affect your ability to spot possible roadblocks and to plan solutions to overcome them.
- *Fail to set progress targets and reviews*
  Long-term goals can keep you going, but having short-term targets keeps you on the right track. Taking time to review your goals and how close you are to them gives you the opportunity to make sure you're still on the right path, and to make changes if you're not.
- *Fail to commit to the business*
  Starting a business takes a lot of time and energy. If you're halfhearted about it, your business won't go anywhere. When you choose to start a business, prepare to sacrifice a lot of your personal time to it. Make sure that your advisors and support network understand your goals and are behind you.

- *Fail to learn from experience*
  Everyone makes mistakes. The key is to learn from them and look for the common error when the same thing keeps going wrong. Don't get trapped by your own stubbornness or pride.
- *Fail to obtain enough startup money*
  Business owners typically overestimate how much they expect to earn and underestimate the costs and length of time they need to get established. Businesses run out of money before they are able to generate their own funds. Be realistic about your startup costs and your likely initial sales. Have backup funds to carry you through rough patches and deal with unexpected expenses.

"I wish I knew how tough things can really get,"

— Marc, age 23, entrepreneur

So how can I succeed?

Getting your business off the ground will require lots of time and hard work, and unexpected setbacks may discourage you from continuing. But don't condemn yourself to failure before you even start. Set realistic goals and allow yourself enough time to achieve them.

Get organized and be prepared for the potential challenges of starting a new business. Research your idea, set goals, make plans, and put what you need together.

CHECKLIST — STARTING A NEW BUSINESS

- Choose a business idea that you enjoy and are passionate about.
- Research the business idea:
  - What will you sell?
  - Is it legal?
  - Who will buy it and how often?
  - Are you willing to do what it takes to sell the product or service?
  - What do you need to deliver the product or service?
  - What will it cost to produce, advertise, sell, and deliver?
  - With what laws will you have to comply?
  - Can you make a profit?
  - How long will it take to make a profit?
- Choose a business name and register the domain name on the Internet, even if you won't use it right away. Register your business name with your provincial and/or federal government.
- Write a business plan and set your business goals.
- Choose a location for the business (e.g., home, office space, storefront).
- Check zoning laws.
- Pick a form of business organization (e.g., sole proprietorship, partnership, or corporation).
- Obtain any required business licences or permits.
- Apply for PST/HST and GST, if required.
- Have business phone or extra residential phone lines installed.
- Get tax information, including record keeping requirements, information on withholding taxes if you will have employees, information on hiring independent contractors, facts about estimating taxes, and forms of organization.
- Open a bank account for the business.
- Have business cards and stationery printed.
- Purchase equipment or supplies.
- Order inventory, signage, and fixtures, as required.
- Get an e-mail address for your business.
- Find a web hosting company and get your website online.
- Prepare marketing materials (e.g., flyers and brochures).

- Call for information about Yellow Pages advertising.
- Place advertising in newspapers or other media, if yours is the type of business that will benefit from paid advertising. Be creative about finding free ways to advertise.
- Call everyone you know and let them know you are in business.

12

Building Your Business Plan

A business plan is a written description of your business and how you expect it to work. It gives an overview of your company and explains what the company does. It also maps out your goals for the future, how you will achieve them, how much they will cost, and how much you'll make. The business plan helps define the company's financial objectives and sums up its business activities.

"A business plan is like a map to success. It keeps you from straying,"

　　　— Damien, 28, entrepreneur and owner of a marketing company

I'm not looking to borrow money from the bank . . .

If you don't plan to borrow money from the bank, you might not see why you should write a business plan. But there are many other reasons for doing a plan.

　　Planning how to make your business work forces

you to think about all the aspects of your business and the problems it might face. Your plan is a map from where you are now, with a great idea and maybe a product to offer, to success — as well as a list of the things you'll need on that journey.

"I didn't need financial help, but after doing the plan, I'm better at selling. My markets are so specific, and I've isolated the language, vocabulary, and selling techniques for each market."

— Helen, 27, business-owner

The business plan helps you to . . .

- figure out where your business needs to go
- predict possible roadblocks along the way
- create responses to those possible roadblocks
- keep the business on track to reach its goals
- get money from outside sources (including loans and grants)
- convince yourself and others that your business can be successful
- see the reality of your ideas, the marketplace, and where your products and services fit.

"I was doubtful about the need for a business plan. You have to justify everything and demonstrate to yourself how this will work. The process of writing the plan changed the direction of my business."

— Derek, 23, entrepreneur

Who is it for?

As the roadmap for your business, it's mainly for you, to keep you on track.

"Until I did it, I didn't understand how useful it was. It made me sit down and focus. I started realizing all the things I needed to know."

— Stephanie, 20, start-up business owner

Of course, many other people will be interested in your plan . . .

- banks, investors, friends, or family — it shows them how you will repay the money you want to borrow
- sales personnel (which may be you at first) — it shows the sales goals you need to reach to turn a profit
- suppliers and manufacturers — it shows them your financial situation, which may help them to give you credits for your supplies.

How does it help?

A good business plan increases your chances for success by making you think seriously about how your business should be run. Also, it can help convince others that you are serious about your ideas and that you know how to make your business work.

> "A business plan gives you structure. It keeps you from spending time and energy on the wrong things."
> — Marco, 22, young entrepreneur

Sometimes when you sit down to work out the details, you realize that you won't be able to reach your goals immediately. Can you really produce 500 necklaces in a week while working out of your house? When you focus on *how* you're going to do things, you revise your goals, make sure they're realistic, and develop strategies so that you won't make unrealistic promises or decisions based on guesswork.

> "When you apply your business plan [to your business], you'll discover problems with it. You plan, you act, then you change your plan."
> — Shanti, 25, young business owner

TIP Before you begin writing your business plan, consider these questions to help focus on the key points:

- What product or service does your business provide, and what needs does it fill?
- Does your product or service have anything special about it or a unique selling point?
- Who are your customers? Is your business idea for everyone, or for a specific group?
- Where will you find your customers? How will you reach them?
- Where will you get the financial resources to start your business? How much will you need?
- What are the costs of making your product or delivering your services?

Do I really need to bother with financials, sales projections, and all that?

The short answer is "maybe not." You *can* simply dive into providing a product or service. But without checking the water, you will find that every time you come up against an obstacle, it will be something you haven't thought of, and you won't know how to cope. The process of sitting down and thinking about every single aspect of your business over the first year, two years, and five years will force you to think about how you are going to get from where you are now to where you want to be. Once you've thought about all the details, you won't face nearly as many surprises or pitfalls.

Writing out all the details *does* seem like a lot of work, especially at the very beginning. If you take each section in stages, though, you may find that it comes together much more easily. Look at each section as a step that takes you closer to having a strong, focused business. Pulling together all the information for your business plan will take time, but it will also help you focus on all the steps you're going to need to make your business a success.

What should I include?

Each business plan is different. Your business isn't going to be exactly like anyone else's, so why would its plan be the same as anyone else's? Remember, this is not a writing contest. It's a written plan to help you be a success. Most business plans do have the same sections.

Executive summary

Although this section is the first thing a reader will read, it's actually the last thing you write — you can't wrap up all the information until first you've written it. Pay the most attention to this section, as it is the first thing everyone will read. Some suggested sections include . . .

- purpose of the business plan
- description of the business
- key products or services that you are providing
- special things about your business that will make you stand out from similar businesses
- clients or customers you are targeting
- financial highlights (you can summarize the highlights in a table)

	Year 1	Year 2
Revenue	$15,000	$25,000
Expenses	$2,000	$3,000
Net profit before tax	$13,000	$22,000

- any special needs your company has (e.g., any equipment that you need in order to get started)
- a description of yourself in a couple of sentences.

Company profile

This section gives the reader an overview of what your company hopes to achieve. Some suggested subheadings include . . .

THE PARTY PEOPLE
Party Planners
**1232 Glencairn Ave.,
Toronto ON, M4R 2F4**

Contents

- *Mission statement*

  Write a couple of sentences describing what your company wants to do and why. For example, the Party People's mission statement might say, "We work with parents and teens to plan fun, cool, safe, themed parties for teenagers. Teens get cool parties; parents can relax, knowing that everyone is safe and that things are under control."

- *Business description*

  This section outlines the concept behind your business and what services you will provide. It also identifies your target market (who you are selling to), and what makes your company unique. The Party People organize food, music, entertainment, and locations for birthdays, graduations, and bar and bat mitzvahs. Their target market is families in their town with major events coming up who want to do something exciting for their teenagers.

- *Industry overview*

  Describe your industry and how your product or service fits into it. For example, what trends affect the industry? Is it new, growing, or stable? The teen party industry isn't new — people have thrown parties for years — however, increasingly, parents want to hand the planning and organizing off to someone else, and teens want a cool party without their parents watching their every move. This part of the entertainment and party planning industry will continue to grow because families are very busy. So in their business plan, the Party People have outlined what the nearest competition does, the differences between planning parties for children and planning parties for teens, and what other industries they have ties to (event venues, catering, and entertainment).

- *Management profile*

  Give a brief description of you and any partners you have. Explain who you are, what you do, the skills and experience that make you qualified for the job. Kyle, the Party People president, was a DJ who provided music at several high school dances and bar and bat mitzvahs. His partner, Sheila, worked as a camp counsellor with teens, and had a part-time job as a youth worker.

Market overview

Your market overview looks at how well your product will sell, and to whom you'll sell it. Some areas to consider include . . .

- *Target market*

  In this customer analysis or breakdown, describe your typical customers (i.e., age, gender, income, where they live, likes and dislikes, etc.) and why they will buy from you. In order to know this, you'll need to do market research — gathering, studying, and analyzing information on what people want and how much they're prepared to spend on it. The Party

People have identified several prospective parties: graduations, sweet sixteens, bar and bat mitzvahs, farewell parties for teens going to college or university, and quinceañeras in the Spanish-speaking community. They know that they have to appeal to the parents as well as to the teens.

- *Competition analysis*

  Think about your competitors and their products. What are their strengths and weaknesses? Who are their customers and how many do they have? Is their product or service priced differently than yours? Describe how your product is unique by comparison. You can organize your findings in a table.

Competitor	Services Offered	Strengths/ Weaknesses	Pricing
TeenTime	Theme parties	Parent-focused; teens don't think their parties are cool	$75/person/party (basic package)

- *Market size*

  Consider the number of potential customers and how much money they spend on similar products. This information is often on the Internet. The Party People know that not all teens' families will pay for their services. However, their business is located in a city with many families, giving them a broad potential customer base.

- *Risk analysis*

  What are the potential risks for your business? Give best and worst case scenarios. A table helps clarify the information.

Risk	Response
Guest getting injured at a party	Make sure all venues have liability insurance. Get liability insurance. Check all venues for hazards prior to party, and teen-proof everything.

- *Market planning*
  State the marketing strategy and the time-related details for carrying it out. Marketing and market planning are discussed further in Chapter 14.

Financial overview

This is where you state how much money you have and what you still need to meet your financial goals. Here are some examples of what to include . . .

- your financial goals — how much money you want your business to be earning within the first year and the first five years
- startup costs, including a list of what you'll need in the first month or two
- sales assumptions, stating how you came up with your sales forecasts
- break-even point — the point at which you'll have made enough to cover your costs but haven't made a profit
- notes to financial statements, explaining any significant assumptions used to put together the cash flow and income statements
- cash flow — shows cash in versus cash out (over 12 months or monthly)
- income statements — shows revenues (how much you've taken in) minus expenses (what you've spent) (two-year forecast, annually), to give an idea of what your earnings (actual income) will be
- sources of financing (if required).

Organization

A brief snapshot of basic information about your company, including . . .

- forms of ownership — are you the only one who owns it (sole proprietor), or is a partnership or a corporation?
- technical assistance — do you have an accountant, lawyer, banker, or mentor?
- insurance — does your business require any type of insurance?
- legal requirements — are there any permits or licences required to operate your business, such as PST or GST number?
- banking — where will you do your banking and who will have the authority to sign cheques?

Appendices

Any additional information, such as financial statements, a startup checklist, research results, résumés, promotional materials, partnership agreements, letters of support, product photos, sample forms you've developed (such as an invoice or sales agreement), and business licence.

How long should my business plan be?

A business plan can be any length, from a few pages to a highly detailed document of 100 pages. It all depends on how you intend to use it, who will see it, and the type of business you plan to start.

"Don't be afraid to write your business plan. It can be short. I avoided writing a plan because I didn't know how to do it. I went to the library and got help. I'm really glad I wrote my plan because now I'm more confident than ever about my business."

— Manuel, 26, entrepreneur

"Make it simple, then apply it."

— Monica, 22, entrepreneur

If you have a simple idea, such as providing childcare, perhaps you can express it in a few pages. However, if you've come up with a new kind of business or are seeking thousands of dollars in startup money, you may have to do a lot of explaining and convincing. Focus on the content of your business plan and be sure it has the right information for the right audience.

Common mistakes when writing a business plan

Even though a business plan is important to their success, a lot of entrepreneurs make these common mistakes that you *can* avoid:

- Procrastinating or dragging your feet. Don't write it the night before you meet with a potential funder. If you need money in six months, put a plan together now. Be prepared to impress funders with a well-researched plan.
- Creating a dull document. Investors and bankers see hundreds of business plans a year. Keep their interest with relevant visuals: charts, tables, bullets, and other graphics. Try to stand out and be creative, if you can.
- Worrying about originality. You're not writing a novel. Investors want a strong plan with dedicated people behind it, not a one-of-a-kind idea.
- Anticipating a million customers. Claim that everyone is your customer and you'll lose credibility. Show that you understand the clients in a smaller market and can serve their needs.
- Emphasizing one big deal. If all or most of your revenue is based on one contract and it falls through, your business could go under. Highlight your company's ability to win other contracts and expand its client base.

- Ignoring the competition. Often, new business owners think their product or service is so terrific that there are no competitors. Be realistic. Show investors that you are prepared to compete in the marketplace.
- Projecting incredible financials. Investors want to see a company with realistic plans for growth. Make sure your numbers are attractive yet reasonable, and include the financial data to back them up.

TIPS FOR A GREAT BUSINESS PLAN

- Keep it short. Stick with the essential facts, and keep the plan focused.
- Use appropriate packaging. You don't need expensive and awkward covers. Basic three-ring and spiral bindings are best.
- Proofread. Read over the plan carefully before you send it to anyone. If possible, have someone else read it over, looking for errors in spelling and grammar. The fewer mistakes you make, the more professional you'll look.

"You can get stuck in the business plan. It needs to be flexible. Get a template, and work from there. The process of making a plan will focus you on what you need to do."

— Colette, 24, freelancer

"Writing a business plan is intimidating. The finished product isn't nearly as important as the process of writing the plan."

— Kevin, 25, young business owner

Get more help

Many books, software programs, and websites that offer templates and can take you through each of the steps involved in writing a good business plan are freely available. The Canada Business Service Centres' website, www.cbsc.org/ibp, has a virtual business planner.

13

Finding the Money

"Hey! I can't afford this on my own!"

Your idea is good; you know what you want to do. Now you have to figure out where to get the money to start your own business, and how to keep yourself going while your business is getting off the ground. If you have some savings it will help. But do you have any other options?

This section is about finding the money you'll need to start your business. Keeping your finances straight should also form part of your business plan, so be sure to read Chapters 12 and 16.

FINANCING is the money raised when a company takes out a loan or sells shares. A FINANCIAL PLAN is a blueprint showing the financial future of a company, including plans for sources of financing and uses for funds.

How much do I need?

Different businesses have different startup demands. A tutoring business, for example, requires very little equipment or space, so the startup costs will be pretty low. A custom upholstery business needs a workspace, and the proprietor will incur costs for tools and materials.

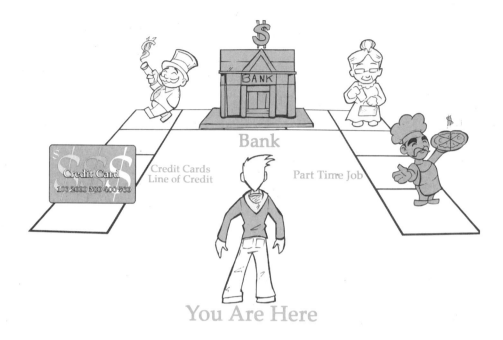

Bank

Credit Cards
Line of Credit

Part Time Job

You Are Here

A realistic financial plan starts with a solid review of what your business costs are likely to be, and forms part of a strong business plan. It's hard to know how much money you're going to need until you need it *right now*. To avoid having to sell your car or computer in order to make a loan payment or to pay off a debt, you should sit down and try to decide how much you'll *really* need.

Make sure you don't set your costs too high or too low. Healthy finances depend on realistic estimates. Set financial goals, and determine how you got your numbers. If your marketing plan requires a flyer campaign across the city, show it in your business plan and budget for it.

To get started, work out both your personal and business budgets. Include a breakdown of all of your costs, from startup costs, monthly bill payments, equipment costs, rent, maintenance of your vehicle, and emergency money in case the water pipes in your store break or you need to have a tooth pulled. Add the two budgets together to figure out how much you need to earn in order to cover both budgets. You might want to take a course in

WHAT ARE YOUR COSTS?

Ask yourself:

- What do I need in order to deliver my product or service?
  - Do I need tools or equipment?
  - Do I need a workspace or office?
  - Do I need materials?
- What about transportation?
- How much do I need to spend on marketing or advertising?
- How will I fill orders? How will I get my product or service to the people who want it?
- How am I going to support myself until my business can support me? Do I need to pay rent? How much do I need to spend on groceries, transportation, and other personal necessities?

financial management to find out how to balance the two. And don't forget that you can also work full- or part-time in order to make ends meet. Just don't lose the focus on your own business.

SHOULD I BUY A FINANCIAL SOFTWARE PACKAGE?

Consider getting a software package to manage your finances. It might seem like a lot of work to learn a new program, but if you get started early, you'll save lots of time later on. Regardless of whether or not you use financial management software, you must keep track of your costs and your business income.

A number of useful software packages can help you with bookkeeping and creating financial statements. Some choices you have include Simply Accounting, MYOB, and QuickBooks. An accounting package can help reduce the time it takes you to enter and manage accounting information and generate financial statements. Although the software package may be a big help, you still need to have a basic understanding of the accounting processes of your company, including what accounting books are used and what general accounts exist. An accounting package can provide the information, but you're the one who needs to know how to analyze a financial statement to make sure that you're meeting your financial goals.

So be honest with yourself. Research how much your product materials and startup are going to cost. Try to factor in changing prices of materials and costs, and leave enough emergency cash for life's curveballs.

What's a budget, and why do I need one?

Here are some of the terms you might need to know:

- A **budget** is a report showing how much you expect to earn (revenue) and how much you will need to spend (expenses) over a specific period of time. If you apply for a loan, you will be expected to have an income statement in order to show that you have planned to earn enough to pay the loan back.
- A **balance sheet** is a status report or snapshot of your financial state at any given time. It shows what your company owns (assets), what it owes (liabilities), and what is left over for you (equity).
- **Break-even sales projections and analysis** are an estimate of what you have to sell in order to cover your expenses. At the "break-even" point in your business, the business has no profits and no losses. Knowing what it will take to break even, and how long, lets you know how to set your pricing in order to meet your needs.
- A **cash flow projection** shows the money going into and out of a business over a specific period of time, including where you get the money and what you will spend the money on. It shows how much money you will have at any given time so that you know how much you need to keep your business going.
- A **financial projection** is a forecast of when you expect to pay your bills based on the expected conditions of your financial position and the results of operations and cash flows. This is an estimate of how much money you are

going to have, based on all of the factors that you know about right now. There is no way to predict if a hurricane is going to occur in the place from where you usually import your shirts. But if you know there's going to be a big surge in sales because you were just interviewed for a top fashion magazine, you can order more of your supplies so that you don't send customers away empty-handed.

- A **statement** is a written report showing how your finances are doing.

Where does money come from?

The short answer is: wherever you can get it. Financing can come from loans (either from a bank, or perhaps from a family member or independent financer), grants (if you can obtain a startup grant from an association, a government agency, an arts council, or a band council), savings (if you have been working for some time and have managed to put some money away), inheritance, sale of an asset (such as a house or car), or in small amounts wherever you can find it.

INVESTMENT (EQUITY) FINANCING comes from people who expect to get some of the benefits of your company through shares or other financial gains. DEBT FINANCING (LOANS) comes from institutions and people who expect the money, plus interest, to be repaid as planned.

Also keep in mind that when you're starting out, you might have to hold a full- or part-time job to pay for your business.

Once you know how much your business is going to need in the first year, you can start looking for the money. You'll also need to consider how much risk you are willing to take — how much money you are comfortable owing — in order to get your business off the ground.

Loans

Loans can come from a traditional lender, such as a bank or credit union, or sometimes from a private lender, such as a family member, a friend, or an agency. The rate of interest and the terms of the loan are likely to be kinder from a friend or family member than they would be from the bank. If you're fortunate enough to be able to borrow money from someone you know in order to capitalize your business, you still need to consider how and when you're going to be able to repay the loan when you're creating your financial plans. Keep in mind that hard feelings may result if your business fails and you can't pay the loan back. If you do borrow from family or friends, treat the loan as a business arrangement, so you can try to keep finances from ruining your relationships.

Most of us don't have wealthy family members just waiting to lend us the capital to make our business dreams come true. So where do we turn?

If you have collateral, such as a car, mortgage, or other items worth money, as well as a decent credit rating, you can approach banks, trusts, and finance companies for a loan. Banks have various types of loans they can offer, such as personal or business lines of credit, business loans, or a second mortgage on a home. Check out different banks' websites for more details on their financing options. You can also try to get a loan or a line of credit from credit unions. Some entrepreneurs feel they are friendlier and more down-to-earth than the banks. Traditional lenders expect the entrepreneur to contribute some of his or her own money, sometimes up to 50 percent of the money needed to start the business. Banks and investment groups also expect entrepreneurs to demonstrate that they are "good risks": people who seem likely to pay the loan money back. It isn't enough to say that you intend to pay the money back — you need to be able to demonstrate that you have a plan that will likely make it possible. This is where your business plan, income statement, and financial projections can help you to convince a lender that your business planning is sound and that your business is a worthwhile investment.

Most young people don't own a house, and they may have student loans to pay off. This makes it hard to borrow money. For many, a part-time or full-time job is the only way to fund a business.

TIP If you have limited or no credit history, you may have trouble getting a loan without a co-signer. To check your credit rating, you can call Equifax Canada at 1-800-465-7166 to order a free credit assessment. You can also visit their website at www.equifax.com/EFX_Canada for more information.

TIP Before applying for a loan, make sure you've put together . . .
- your business plan, which is one of your most important tools to obtain a loan
- your business's cash flow projections (see page 150 for more info on cash flow projections)
- a personal financial statement.

You might want to consider government loan programs, such as a government Business Improvement Loan (SBLA) for the purchase of fixed assets. This loan is government guaranteed and can be accessed through the major banks. The Business Development Corporation (BDC) offers technology- and export-related loans, in addition to administering youth and microlending programs. Check out their website at www.bdc.ca.

FIXED ASSETS, also called PLANT, refers to property such as land, buildings, equipment, and furniture that is used in the operation of a business and is not expected to be sold in the upcoming year.

Some places offer special loan funds specifically for people wanting to start their own businesses. The Canadian Youth Business Foundation grants loans of up to $15,000 for entrepreneurs under 30.

Research your choices for different types of loans on the Internet. Or if you know someone who started their own business, ask how they got the money. Most large cities have business enterprise centres that can help with finding the money.

> TIP Many entrepreneurs don't get funding the first time they try. You need to keep trying and ask for help. If your first choice financial institution turns you down, ask why the loan was rejected. Remember that each time you apply for a bank loan, the application shows up on your credit rating. The next bank may ask more questions. You could try approaching a bank officer informally. Show your plan, and get an opinion without formally applying for a loan.

You may have success approaching private investors, who are also known as "Angels." They can invest up to $250,000, although the typical amount is $100,000, usually in technology-based products. Private investors can be found through accountants, lawyers, and networking groups.

But I don't want to start out with a debt. Is there any other way to get money?

Since young entrepreneurs often aren't the ideal candidates for loans from the lender's point of view, you may find that you just can't convince anyone to lend you the money you need when you're just starting your business. You may simply not want to start your business with a debt. So how do you find money without taking out a loan?

"A friend of mine borrowed $10,000 from the bank to get her business started, and that's great for her — she can live with the *debt. But I couldn't live with a debt like that hanging over my head. I don't want to start with my business owing money to anyone. So I'm working part-time, which is tiring, but it means that any money my business makes is for the business — I don't have to pay it back."*

— Rosa, 26, artist and entrepreneur

Your business may qualify for grants, or you may have to wait until your savings can cover your business expenses, or work part-time to support yourself and your business.

Grants

Several government programs and agencies provide grants to entrepreneurs who meet specific criteria. While applying for grants can be time consuming, the payout can make the effort well worth it — and you don't have to pay a grant back. Check out the Business Guide to Government Programs at www.businessguide.net to get an idea of what's available.

Savings

Some entrepreneurs launch their businesses after working at another job or on contracts for other businesses, and saving the money they'll need to start their business. While it may be frustrating working for someone else when you're itching to sell your ideas and talent to the world, spending some time learning from other businesses and saving the money can put you in a better financial position. Working for someone else can give you the opportunity to learn about a related industry, or about business and management in general.

Your business

The capital you need may come out of your business activities. You can ask your customers for a deposit for services or products they order from you, and use the money to purchase supplies and inventory. You can try bartering — exchanging your services for services or products that you need. For example, your company could design a website for an accountant, who then could provide bookkeeping services to your company.

Credit cards

As a last resort, you can use your credit card to pay your startup expenses. However, approach credit with caution! High interest combined with a large balance can put a strain on your business's finances. If you find that you need to use credit, use it only to make small purchases, so that you can easily pay the balance. Paying off your balance monthly will help build a good credit rating. Also, try to find a credit card with a low interest rate. Avoid store credit cards, whose rates can be as high as 30 percent.

FIVE Cs OF CREDIT

Conditions: Is there a good operating environment in your industry?

Character: Will you be able to run the business?

Capacity to repay: Will the company make enough profit to pay back the loan easily?

Collateral: What security is being offered against the loan (e.g., mortgage, car)?

Capital: What is your investment in the business?

Should I work for someone else?

A regular job may provide the steady income you need while you're getting your business off the ground.

While a part-time job may cover your living expenses, it can drain the time and energy you have available for your business. Starting a business can take more time than a full-time job, so adding part-time hours to your already full workweek may be too demanding. However, if your business is slow getting started, and you're not making enough from it to cover your business costs and keep eating at the same time, working part time can provide you with an alternative to debt. If your part-time job covers your living expenses, any earnings from your business can go directly back into the business.

While it's possible to start a business while working full time, many entrepreneurs find that there just aren't enough hours in the week to work full-time hours for an employer and for themselves. "Only having a part-time job is important, because you can't focus on your business if you're working full time for someone else," says Jennifer, who found grants to fund her business while working part-time in retail, and turned down a full-time job offer in order to work on her business.

> "A job in the service industry, like serving or bartending, is good because you have a quick return. You make more money for less amount of hours of working."
>
> — Don, 25, owner of a bike-repair service

Consider finding a part-time job in the industry where you want to start your own business. You can use this experience to learn more about that industry and make industry contacts. If you do choose to work in your industry, be careful to avoid competing with your employer — getting yourself into a kind of situation where your employer sees you as competition may damage your reputation in the long run.

Take as much knowledge as you can from any jobs you may have to do, and apply it to your own business. Even if you are not crazy about what you're doing, look at it as getting paid to learn firsthand about some part of running a business.

Wow, that's a lot! How can I reduce my startup costs?

Wouldn't it be great if you could start your business with lottery winnings? Unfortunately, most young entrepreneurs don't have large amounts of cash at their disposal. The tough reality is that you have to finance your own way; cutting corners and putting all your earnings back into your business (also known as bootstrapping) is the only way to survive the early stages.

Examine all of your costs to see if you need as much as you think you do. Bootstrapping makes sense when other ways of getting cash are unavailable. Successful entrepreneurs are masters at stretching every dollar.

TIP Another option to keep in mind is tax credits. Find out if your chosen industry offers any sort of programs that can give you a break at tax time.

You can find many ways to cut corners. Just make sure cost-cutting doesn't damage the quality of the product you're selling or limit your business. Learning how to make necessary and sometimes painful cuts is important. Here are some tips to help you survive on a shoestring budget:

- Try to keep your overhead low. Work out of home, if you can. Don't be in a rush to rent an office or workspace, if you don't need one right now for your business.
- Some cities have low-rent incubator offices, where for a small fee you get a shared space in an office, with phone, Internet, photocopier, and fax. Search on the Internet for an incubator office in your area.
- Most new businesses don't require top-of-the-line equipment and cutting-edge technology. Take advantage of that old computer or makeshift workbench until it is no longer useful. Replace equipment and technology only when it's absolutely necessary. Even then, try to buy used equipment rather than new.
- Try to negotiate payment terms with the supplier of the materials you need to make your product. Suppliers usually want cash on delivery (COD) from start-ups, but someone might give you credit with a down payment up front.
- Buy used office furniture or equipment from leasing companies or thrift shops. Read the classified ads for sales, auctions, and liquidations. If you know people with their

own businesses, find out if they're planning to upgrade their equipment and buy their used equipment.

- Try to negotiate time rather than price. If you find your vendors and suppliers won't budge on prices, try to get payment extensions. Ask if you can pay bills on 45-, 60- or 90-day terms, instead of the standard 30 days. This allows you to build cash flow and working capital.

- Research and sign up for the best long-distance calling plan you can find, and try to limit your long distance calls to off-peak times. Don't be afraid to switch, or threaten to switch, long-distance providers to get a better deal. If you're working from home, don't order a business telephone or fax line. A residential line can be one-quarter the cost of a business line and serve the same purpose. Also, call your phone company to see if you can bundle long distance, cellular, and Internet access into one less expensive package.

- Monitor energy consumption in your home and workspace. Use auto-setback thermostats and automatic light switches. You may save more than you expect.

- If you can't afford to buy the big equipment you need, such as a photocopier, high-speed computer, or car, consider leasing the equipment instead. That way, you can lease-to-own the equipment, making small payments every month instead of one big payment off the top. After all the payments have been made, the equipment is yours to keep.

- Put as much money as possible into working assets (inventory and working capital), which bring in sales and cash, and as little as possible into fixed assets (real estate, furnishings, and equipment).

- Build up sales as quickly as you can. Spend at least two hours each day on marketing and sales. Figure out how you're going to get those paying customers before you open, so you can increase your sales right away.
- Master your finances and financial tools. Know every aspect of your business, including marketing, production, and finances. This will give you control over your business's direction. You need to understand your cash flow, income, profit and loss statements, and break-even point so you can tell where you've been, where you're going, and how fast you're getting there.

Bootstrapping isn't easy. It requires discipline, diligence, and hard work. Don't expect everything to fall into place right away. No matter how tough things get, stay focused on your mission: to successfully start your business.

TIP You'll need to open a business account at a bank to keep all the money you're going to earn from your new company. Your own bank may be a good place to start. Or ask for advice and references from other small businesses. Since you're just starting out, you probably won't have much money. Before approaching different banks, think about what your banking needs will be. Do you need lock-box services, overdraft protection, and online and telephone banking, or will just a deposit account do? When you do approach different banks, ask if they offer commercial loans for businesses, or check out their websites for more information on the services they provide. Also ask about getting a non-interest-bearing chequing account that has little or no fees. Once you know what you need from your bank, it will be easier to decide which bank offers the best service for your business. Remember, it's a good idea to establish a relationship with a banker before you need money. The right banker will understand the needs of new and growing businesses. They will be interested in your business dreams, and will help you achieve them.

14

Marketing

What is marketing?

You can have the greatest product in the world, but if nobody knows about it, nobody will buy it. So how do you get the word out? You *market* your product. Marketing is the process of researching who will buy your product or service, informing those people that it is for sale, creating an appealing package, and making it available to the customers.

MARKETING VERSUS ADVERTISING

Many people confuse **marketing** with **advertising**. Although marketing does involve advertising, you can sell and promote what you do in many ways.

Marketing refers to the entire process of making sure the people who are likely to buy a product or service know what it is and how to get it, and that the product or service appeals to that group of people. It includes market research and packaging as well as reaching out to the people who will buy your product or service.

Advertising is often the most obvious marketing activity. It consists of paid announcements that call public attention to a product or service through publications, billboards, direct mail, and broadcasting on television or radio.

But I just want to make my product. Why should I market my business?

Sure, once people know what you do, they'll probably want to buy it from you. But it's up to you to tell them what you have to offer. If you don't market your business, your business won't grow.

Often, entrepreneurs don't really know who is likely to buy their product or service, or the best way to make people aware of it. Advertising is expensive, so you want to make sure that you focus any advertising on the correct group of people. There are also a number of less expensive ways to get the word out to the people who are likely to buy what you're selling. Market research will help you find out who will pay for your product or service. Once you know who will buy it, then those people need to know that your product or service exists, and how to get it.

Okay . . . I'm convinced that marketing is important. So do I start advertising?

Advertising is one marketing activity; it's not the first step. Good marketing is *targeted* and *planned*. Just as you researched your business idea, now you need to research the market for your business. By conducting market research, you will be able to figure out how to focus your attention on those most likely to buy your product or service (your "target market"), which will boost your sales and save you time and money.

Your MARKET is the group of people who will buy your product or service. MARKET RESEARCH is gathering information to help identify your market and learn how best to convince it to buy your product or service.

"Market research helps you define your customers, and keeps you from wasting time. Do surveys. Talk to people, and know your audience."

— Vaughan, 22, entrepreneur and designer

"Sometimes your best market is not the market you thought you wanted. You may be surprised."

— Clarissa, 27, small business owner

Market research helps you learn . . .

- who your customers are and what they want
- how to reach your customers
- which advertising techniques work the best and which get no response
- how to avoid repeating mistakes.

"Market research is like stepping lightly on a frozen pond to see if the ice will hold your weight."

— Jason, 25, caterer

Where do I start?
Your market research will help you identify how your product or service fits in the market.

Where do I find this information?
You can use secondary sources such as books, other companies' annual reports, and web pages to find some of the information you'll need. To answer other questions, you'll need to talk to your potential customers and your competition. Secondary sources are easier to access and cheaper than primary sources, so get as much information as you can from them.

Customer Research
Create a market survey for customers. A survey can take place by phone, in person, by mail or e-mail, or using a combination. Your market survey should be clear, concise, and take no more than 10 minutes. It should help you to figure out who wants to buy your

product or service, where they shop, how much they're likely to spend, and what they respond best to. You can also survey current customers to find out how well your product or service met their needs and lived up to their expectations.

Competitor Research

You can also do a competitor survey by visiting your competitor's store, calling for prices and services, interviewing indirect competitors (companies that don't sell the same product or service but offer the same results), or visiting trade shows in order to figure out how to price your own product.

TIP Ask the librarian at your public library for research help. Librarians are excellent at finding information in places you might not think to look.

To plan your marketing, your research will need to answer these questions:

Is there a need for your product or service?

If nobody needs what you are selling, is it something anyone is likely to buy?

Who is your market?

Who buys what you have to sell? Are most of your customers male or female? How old are they? How much money do they earn every year? How much do they spend on the product or service you are offering?

You can gather this information from government studies, chambers of commerce, trade associations, the annual reports of your competition, and other organizations.

Where do your customers shop?

How do your potential customers find out about similar products or services? Do they shop online? In malls? Through catalogues? Do they respond to promotional offers? Visit websites that sell similar products or services, and research these companies' sales. Survey your potential customers to find out how they shop.

Why do your customers buy?

What is your target customer looking for when they buy a product like yours? Are you offering a service that will meet their needs? A product that will fit their wardrobes? Do they want to be entertained, fed, or made to look good?

How much do your customers buy?

How much do people in your market spend, annually, on products or services similar to the ones you have to offer? Are your customers likely to buy frequently, or once in a while? Knowing how much people spend on what you're selling will let you know how much of a market there is for what you're offering, and give you an idea of whether it's a market you can break into.

Who are your competitors?

Look around you, in the phone book, and on the web. Who is offering products or services similar to what you're offering? Are they in direct competition with you?

Your DIRECT COMPETITORS offer the same product or service that you do. Customers looking for what you offer will have to choose between similar products. For example, if you run a catering business, other caterers in your area offering the same sort of food are your direct competition.

Your INDIRECT COMPETITORS don't necessarily sell the same products, but they offer the same results to the customer. Indirect competition for a caterer might include eat-in restaurants that offer catering or take-out services, grocery stores, and companies that sell ready-made hors d'oeuvres.

How much does the competition charge?

Visit competing businesses, if you can, or phone to find out about prices and services offered in order to figure out how to price your own product or service. Talk with other members of your industry and find out what they charge.

How much should you charge?

When you create your customer survey, find out how much people are willing to pay for your product or service. Look at what the competition charges. Look at how much it costs you to produce your product or perform your service. Set your price list so that you are covering your costs and generating profit, but not pricing yourself out of the market by selling your product or service for more than your competition.

How can you best promote your business?

How do your customers find out about products or services? Do they search the web? Do they read trade magazines? Are they coupon-clippers?

Once you've tallied the results of your customer surveys and your competition research, you should have a clear idea of how best to market your product or service. Use this information to create your marketing plan.

"Busy people are a lot more accessible than you might think. I found a lot of people were really happy to answer my questions and give me their time."

— Leah, 29, owner of a start-up business

MARKETING MUSTS . . .

- market research
- networking
- business cards
- voice mail
- sales
- customer service

A trade show is a convention where advertising agencies and other companies within related industries show and compare products, services, and ideas to retailers and other potential customers. Relevant trade shows can be good places to market your business, because they give you a chance to reach a large number of people at one time. Before exhibiting at a trade show, be certain you can fill large orders for your product.

You can also attend a trade show to meet people doing work similar to yours. So even if you're not ready to exhibit your business, you can approach other people in the industry to find out what they did when they first started out.

Other people in your industry, as well as industry or trade associations, can often tell you about trade shows. You can also search on the Internet for local listings.

I've done the research. Do I advertise now?

Not yet. You've targeted your market, now you need to *plan* how to let that market know your business exists.

MARKETING STRATEGIES are specific tactics or methods used to attract attention to your company and get more customers. A MARKETING PLAN is your guide to how to proceed with your marketing strategies. They combine to make the MARKETING MIX, also known as the FOUR Ps OF MARKETING: Price, Place, Product, and Promotion. Varying the "mix" can help you to reach different segments of your market.

To help you figure out what to include in your marketing plan, this section describes the parts of a plan and what they contain. To begin, here's a sample of a marketing plan:

TONY'S LAWN CARE SERVICE

Overall Objectives ◄————

- Obtain 15 clients in the first year.
- Inform potential customers that a lawn care service is available right in the neighbourhood.
- Establish a client base that will spread the word of the good service they receive.

> State how you are reaching your market right now and how many customers you have. Set sales goals for the month, six months, or year.

Market Research ◄————

- There are approximately 2,000 houses with lawns in this neighbourhood.
- Average household income in this neighbourhood is $50,000/year.
- A drive through the neighbourhood shows that at least five lawns on every street could certainly *use* regular cutting, watering, and fertilizing. Lots of people also have gardens that could use some care.

> Discuss what the information you collected tells you about target markets, competition, current sales, and suppliers.

Of 100 residents surveyed . . .

- 52 said they do their own lawn care and gardening at least once a week, and never use help.
- 22 said they could use help when they're away or very busy.
- 10 said they don't think much about lawn care but could probably use some help.
- 10 said they pay a student to cut the lawn.
- Six said they use a lawn care service.

- Of the residents who use lawn care service, three are happy with the service they use, and three are not.
- Of those who are not happy, two said the service was unreliable, one said it was expensive.

- Of the residents who pay a student, four said they were happy, and six said they weren't. Two of these said they'd pay more for better service.

- Therefore, out of 100 people surveyed, Tony's Lawn Care might find five customers. If the survey represents all the people in the neighbourhood, he could have 100 customers in this neighbourhood. It's not likely that all people who might use lawn care services will use Tony's.
- Tony also has six customers from previous summers who wish to continue using his services.

Competition ←

Figure out who is in direct and indirect competition with your business, how much they charge, and how they reach their market.

- Greenlawns, Inc., a city-wide lawn care and landscaping service, is the professional competition. They charge $20/hour. They have bus ads, flyers, and signs on the lawns they take care of.
- There is no lawn-care professional in this neighbourhood.
- Many people who might use lawn care use students, who usually charge $8–$10/hour.

Target Markets ←

Define target markets (i.e., by age, gender, profession, income level, education level, and/or residence) for your product and describe them.

- Seniors with disposable income
- Professionals without children who are always travelling or working
- People with large yards that are neglected because they're hard to manage (trees, shrubs, finicky plants, too many weeds)

Product

- Tony's services are much cheaper than those of professionals, so customers can afford to have their lawn cut and tended to every week instead of every second week.
- The business is neighbourhood focused — Tony knows the trouble with lawn care in the neighbourhood because he's taken care of his family's lawn and garden for years.

> Describe your product. Develop your "unique selling point." What makes you stand apart from your competition?

Marketing Strategy

- Create a flyer to distribute to all the houses from Clarence Avenue to Preston Avenue.
- Post a flyer at the grocery store.
- Of those residents who pay a student, four of them were unhappy with the service they were getting but were unwilling to pay more for better service. Try winning them over with a promotional three-week trial offer at the price they're used to paying in the hopes they'll become regular customers after they see the work.
- Ask current clients to spread the word about the new service available in the neighbourhood.

> Describe all the methods you will use to achieve your objectives.

Pricing and Positioning

No one living in the neighbourhood provides this service. Tony will charge $15/hour for mowing and any additional care required, such as weeding, hedge trimming, and pruning, and extra costs for providing seeds and fertilizer will be negotiated with the client before the work is started.

> Establish strategies for determining the price of your product or service and where it will be positioned in the market.

Budget

- Marketing budget is very small to non-existent.
- Create the flyer on the computer. Tony's mom's employer has offered to let him use her photocopier for

> Budget your money, splitting costs into what you can do yourself and what you need to hire someone else to do.

3¢ a copy (total cost for 600 flyers: $100, because he's printing two per page and cutting the paper in half).

- Ask current clients to spread the word next time Tony comes to mow their lawns. Create free business cards using Internet business card service, and leave them with current clients.

Monitor Results

Survey customers; ask if they'd recommend his services to someone else. When people call for his services, ask how they heard about the company. Keep track of whether the flyers are working, or if it's through word-of-mouth. Track the amount of earnings in a spreadsheet, and put excess into a high interest savings account. Keep a list of people who might be interested when they go on vacation, and send them occasional reminder flyers that this service is available.

> Test and analyze results. Identify useful strategies, survey customers. Track sales and leads.

Overall objective

Start your marketing plan with an objective stating where you are now and where you want to go in the future. Give a specific timeframe (e.g., next three months, one year, 10 years) for what you hope to achieve. Set up realistic objectives and goals that you can turn into numbers. For instance, your goal might be to gain at least 15 new clients in a year, or to sell 10 products per week.

When deciding on marketing objectives, ask yourself . . .

- How many customers do you need in the first three months, six months, and year to succeed?
- Will your service be available only in a specific area, or will you branch out to other areas? Can you afford to ship your product to other cities or countries?

Marketing strategies

Next, come up with some marketing strategies, including all the methods you will use to achieve your objectives. Focus on bringing the product to the attention of your customers. Some strategies to think about include . . .

- networking — go where your market is and tell people what you do
- direct marketing — brochures, flyers
- advertising — print media, directories
- direct/personal selling — phone potential customers and ask them how you can best meet their needs
- publicity/press releases — write an interesting press release and send it to people who may be interested
- trade shows — even if you don't yet have enough business to set up a display, go with your business cards and company information and talk to people
- website — make certain that your company shows up in search engines
- word-of-mouth — do good work, and your customers and clients will happily tell other people about you.

Pricing and positioning

From the information you've collected, establish strategies for determining the price of your product and where your product will be positioned in the market.

Budget

Figure out how much money you have to spend on promoting your business. Some questions to ask yourself: What can you afford to do? What can you do yourself? What do you need to hire someone to do?

Monitor results

And finally, you'll need to monitor the results of your marketing plan. Every time you get a new customer or client, ask how they found out about you. You can also track sales, leads, and visitors to your website. Focus on the strategies that are working best for you.

It's time to advertise!

You have a marketing plan in place, you know who your target market is, how you can reach them, and how much money you have to advertise. Now it's time to let those people know you're up and running and ready for their business.

"I had to figure out: How do I get business cards made? What about hits on my website? How can I get publicity for cheap?"

— Bill, 20, entrepreneur

How do I promote my business on a tight budget?

You need to get the word out about your business, but you probably don't have a large advertising budget. Some good — and cheap — tools you can use to market your product include . . .

- logos, letterhead, flyers, posters, brochures — create them yourself, or ask an artistic or computer-savvy friend for help
- newspaper classified ads
- coupon mail packs — shop around for the best deal
- sidewalk footsteps to your storefront or stand — bring the customers to your doorstep
- window banners/displays — showcase special deals you have to offer
- free trial offers, sampling, two-for-one offers, contests — use different promotions to get customers interested and talking about your product or service
- word-of-mouth.

"I'm seeing firsthand the power of word-of-mouth. My current clients want to be on board without seeing my portfolio."

— Ian, 24, freelance graphic artist

"Promotion is key to any business. If no one knows you're there providing a service, how will they know they need it?"

— Stan, 25, Reiki practitioner

ADVERTISING DOs AND DON'Ts

Visit the Canada Business Service Centre website, www.cbsc.org/ontario, for a list of advertising dos and don'ts, as well as other useful information about marketing and starting your own business.

15

Operations: The Everyday Details of Running Your Business

"What do I need to know to keep things running smoothly?"

Your business is up and running. You have customers, you have a product or service, and you're delivering on your orders. That's great. Unfortunately, it's not everything. You need to keep on top of the financial details of running your business.

Why do I need to do financials?

Financials are the tools that you will use to track the money coming in and out of your business. Entrepreneurs often find the financial side the most challenging part of running a business. They don't understand why they need to do a budget or balance sheet, or how to handle projections. But knowing how much money you're making, how much you're spending, and the details of where it's coming from and going to makes it easier to plan your year, to approach potential lenders or investors, and to deal with your taxes.

While this section will give you an outline of how to figure out your finances and what tools you can use, a wealth of information is available on the Internet or in books at the library. Also, many computer programs exist to help small-business owners manage their finances and taxes.

A BUDGET is an organized plan for spending a fixed resource (money) during a specific period of time.

How can I plan ahead so that my business provides the income I need?

A budget is the tool you use for planning what you expect to make in the upcoming year and what you expect your expenses to be. Budgets are very simple to make: list all your expected income, then list all your expected expenses. If your expected income is more than your expected expenses, you'll be making a profit on the year. If the expenses are higher, you'll lose money. Keep tinkering with the budget (usually by shaving costs) until it shows you making the amount of profit you need to make. Then use the budget as a road map for the year.

How do I know if my budget is on track?

Budgets are great for planning, but you have to watch closely to make sure you are staying within your budget. You do this with an **income statement**, also called a **profit and loss** or **P&L**. This statement shows your total sales and other income to date, as well as all of your costs. It shows how much the business has made (or lost) in the year to date. Many income statements also show the budget for that period, and show how the actual income and expenses vary from what had been planned. If the business is not doing as well as expected, the income statement will show where it has gone off the rails.

If you plan on applying for a loan, have your budget and income statement ready for your investors to show how you plan to pay the money back.

My business is on budget but I don't have enough money to pay my bills. What is going wrong?

Even very healthy businesses sometimes have problems with **cash flow**. Even if the business is making a large annual profit, it is not unusual for the expenses to fall due before the money has come in.

Most businesses need to prepare cash flow projections. A **cash flow projection** is a plan (much like a budget) that tracks when money is expected to come in and when it will need to go out to pay expenses. The purpose of the projection is to let you spot periods when you won't have enough money available to pay your commitments. If you spot problems like that ahead of time, you can plan ways of avoiding them (by delaying purchases or arranging financing).

Knowing when you will have money coming in, and when you will have to make payments, helps you to . . .

- make sure you have enough cash to purchase the materials or stock that you need
- take advantage of special discounts on supplies
- plan to buy or upgrade equipment
- prepare for required future financing and determine the type of financing you need (line of credit, long-term debt)
- impress lenders with your ability to repay them on time.

How do I know if my cash flow projection isn't on track?

As with the budget, you need to know if your cash flow plan is working. But problems with the budget can be subtle, and often take a while to become obvious. Problems with a cash flow projection become obvious immediately: if you are off track, you don't have the money you need to pay your bills!

The tool used to track how well your cash flow planning is going is called a **statement of cash flow**. It shows how the money entered and left your bank account. And it will pinpoint where your plans have gone wrong, so that you can address the problem.

("Addressing the problem" usually means cutting back on your spending for a while or phoning people who owe you money and bugging them to pay you.)

How do I know if my business is doing okay?

A **balance sheet** gives you a clear picture of where your business stands, including its strengths and where it needs to improve. It lists the **assets** (anything the business owns that is worth money, including furniture, equipment, and cash in the bank), **liabilities** (money owed, such as taxes and unpaid bills), and, most important, the **equity**, which is what the business is worth.

A company whose equity is a negative number is (at least technically) bankrupt.

An easy equation for a balance sheet is Assets = Liabilities + Equity.

Here's how it works. To get the assets, add up all the cash in bank accounts, the value of investments, the value of all your business's property — including furniture, equipment, and vehicles, minus depreciation — plus whatever is owed to you. To get your liabilities, figure out what you owe in loans, credit cards, and unpaid bills. Subtract your liabilities from your assets to get your equity.

If I sold my assets, would I get back what I paid?

You most likely wouldn't get all the money back, because some assets **depreciate** in value. This means that their value goes down because of age, wear, or market conditions. Check out the instructions on your business tax form under Capital Cost Allowance for information on how to figure out depreciation of your property.

How do I set my prices?

If you don't charge enough to cover the costs of your materials, your overhead, and your time, the business will lose money and you'll be unable to pay the bills. If you charge too much, customers may not want to buy your product. So setting realistic prices is important.

The **break-even point** in your business is when your sales cover your costs. **Break-even sales projections** and **analyses** help you figure out how to price your product or service in order to reach the break-even point.

The formula is pretty simple: Total fixed costs or overhead divided by (price per unit minus variable costs per unit) equals sales at the break-even point. For example, you calculate that your candle-making company has a fixed overhead of $4,500 a year (which covers rent and electric bills). It costs $3 per candle to make, advertise, and deliver the candles. That is your variable cost. Based on your market research, you think you can easily sell each candle for $12.

$$\$4{,}500 \div (\$12 - \$3) = 500$$

You need to sell 500 candles to break even. Every candle you sell after the 500th makes you a $9 profit.

Do I need to give out invoices and receipts?

You will need to send invoices to your customers so that they have a record of how much to pay you, when the money is due, and what product or service they are paying you for. You need to issue receipts to your customers to show that they have paid you for your product or service.

How do I prepare invoices and receipts?

If you're computer-savvy, you can use software to make your own invoices. They don't need to be fancy; just make sure they include the information you need, such as . . .

- the date
- the service provided
- who did the work
- how much is owed
- any applicable taxes.

You can also use a receipt pad, type the receipts, or print them from a register or a calculator with a printer function. A receipt should state the name of your business, the item or service, the price, any taxes that apply, the amount due, and the amount paid.

What is inventory? Why should I bother keeping track of it?

Inventory is a detailed list of everything you have in stock, including merchandise, raw materials, and unfinished and finished products that have not been sold. You need to keep track of what went out and what came in so that you know what is selling, when it sells, and if you need to stock any more or less of a certain item. You can do this either with inventory books or a spreadsheet on your computer.

How will I know what to do about taxes?

Your business has taxes to pay in addition to the personal taxes that you pay every year. Taxes don't need to be scary or annoying, but you have to plan for them and pay them on time.

TIP Collect and organize all of your relevant receipts as you go. Remember: for tax purposes, you must keep all of your receipts and records for six years.

The taxes you pay depend on the type of company you have (sole proprietorship, partnership, or corporation). To find out which business taxes apply to you, check with your province's or territory's Ministry of Finance.

What if I don't pay my taxes?

Nobody likes paying taxes. But it isn't optional. If you don't pay your taxes on time, the government will charge interest on the amounts that you owe. If you continue to avoid paying your taxes, you may be charged with serious fines or wind up in jail. So it's worthwhile to keep your taxes and paperwork up-to-date and organized. If the Canada Revenue Agency (CRA) decides to audit your business, they will want to see all of your bookkeeping to make sure it is accurate and complies with applicable laws, regulations, and policies. The best way to avoid problems with the CRA is to keep clear, organized records and to file your taxes as scheduled.

HOW MUCH SHOULD I SET ASIDE FOR TAXES?

Remember to set aside at least 20 percent of your **profits** (not of your total income) for tax purposes. You don't want all that money you've earned to be taken away by the CRA, so file and pay your taxes on time.

What is the difference between GST, PST, and HST?

The Goods and Services Tax (GST) is a 7 percent sales tax on most Canadian products and services. Many provinces also have a Provincial Sales Tax (PST) on some products and services. The Harmonized Sales Tax (HST) applies in the provinces of Nova Scotia, New Brunswick, and Newfoundland, where they have combined the PST with the GST for a total of 15 percent tax.

In Quebec, the Ministère du Revenu du Québec (MRQ) administers the GST and HST for the CRA. You can contact the MRQ toll-free at 1-800-567-4692.

Do I have to register for GST/HST?

Not necessarily. Your product or service may be exempt from GST or HST, which means you would not have to collect and send the GST or HST to the CRA. Examples of exempt services are music lessons and childcare services. Some goods, such as basic groceries like milk and bread, are considered "zero-rated goods" and do not require GST or HST registration. You may not have to register if you qualify as a small supplier according to the CRA. To see if you are considered a small supplier, contact the CRA at 1-800-959-5525 or check out their website at www.cra-arc.gc.ca.

Dealing with the GST/HST can be time-consuming. As a consumer, you have to pay it. As a business person, you may have to collect it and give it to the CRA. By registering, you make sure that you get back as much as possible of the GST or HST that you've paid out.

TIP You are required to register for GST or HST if you make $30,000 or more before expenses for four consecutive quarters or for any single quarter.

What is a Vendor Permit? Do I need one?

You require a Vendor Permit to charge, collect, and remit PST on your taxable sales. You **must** obtain a PST Vendor Permit if you regularly sell taxable goods, even if your sales are small. Unlike the GST registration, there is no minimum amount. You also need to keep a copy of your Vendor Permit at each business location and let anyone see it on request.

You do **not** need a Vendor Permit if:

- you sell only tax-exempt goods, such as fresh fruit and vegetables at a roadside stand
- you provide only non-taxable services, such as dry cleaning or consulting
- you are a wholesaler or manufacturer and do not make retail sales
- you do business in provinces or territories that don't have provincial sales taxes (Alberta, Yukon, Nunavut, or the Northwest Territories).

Exactly which goods and services are taxable varies from province to province, so check your province's Ministry of Finance web page. Although many provinces call PST Retail Sales Tax (RST), it doesn't apply only to retail businesses, so check the lists of taxable businesses to see whether your specific product or service is taxable.

TIP If you determine that you need a GST/HST account, register for an account using Business Registration On-line at www.businessregistration. gc.ca. You can also register for a new Business Number (BN), as well as apply for new Ontario, Nova Scotia, New Brunswick, and British Columbia program accounts, including PST, at this website.

WHAT IS A . . .

- **trademark?** A word, symbol, design, or a combination of these features used by a company to distinguish itself or its merchandise. Laws can protect a registered trademark from misuse and imitation.
- **copyright?** The right to create and distribute copies of a literary, artistic, dramatic, or musical work. Only the owner of copyright is allowed to produce or reproduce the work or to permit anyone else to do so.
- **patent?** The sole right, granted by the government, to sell, use, and manufacture an invention or creation. To patent a device, you must prove that it is useful, original, and not obvious.

For more information on trademarks, copyrights, and patents, visit the Canadian Intellectual Property Office website at www.strategis.ic.gc.ca/ engdoc/main.html.

16

Secrets for Success

"So what are the secret ingredients?"

You have your business plan, you've done your market research, and you have a few customers. You're on your way. So how do you turn a good start into a successful business?

You want the time, effort, and money you've put into your business to pay off. You want your business to make enough money to support you, you want a solid base of customers or clients, and you want your business to grow.

During the first few years, you're going to pour a lot of time into creating your business, but success usually comes slowly, one little victory at a time. Your first couple of years will be about building as many victories as you can, and learning from your mistakes.

To make it easier to succeed, you need to set up your business and your life in ways that give you the time to focus on your business and the freedom to make mistakes. This means . . .

- having enough capital (money) to let you do things right and not always be scrambling to pay the bills
- having support from friends and family, who understand that you're going to have a lot on the go over the next year or two

- learning to manage your time effectively so that you can do your best work and still have time for your personal life
- setting realistic prices for your product or service so that you can cover your expenses and have some earnings to put back into your business.

TIP One key to success is self-discipline. When you're the boss, sometimes it's too easy to make allowances for your personal life. You need to be clear on what parts of your day are work and what parts of your day are free for friends, family, or relaxing.

What happened to my life? All I do is work!

Balancing your new business and your personal life may not be easy, especially if you're working at another job at the same time. Know going in that your personal life is probably going to suffer, and don't make too many commitments for the first year or so.

Of course, this doesn't mean you should neglect your friends and family, or that you should work until you're sick. But if you want to be up early for meetings, for example, you may need to start meeting your friends for lunch rather than partying until late at night.

Your business will demand as much time as you can put into it. Remember, though, that you're going to need a support network, so don't completely ignore your friends and family while you're pouring yourself into work. Remember to keep some time to hang out, go to the gym, or read a book — you need to in order to maintain your sanity.

"Don't isolate yourself. Keep in contact, keep moving. Have a support person you can talk to."

— Manuel, 24, new business owner

Manage your time

If you're trying to get a new business off the ground while juggling lots of other things, such as a full- or part-time job and family duties, you need a plan to help you get everything done. If you get organized and set priorities, you'll be well on your way to managing your time and avoiding headaches.

DOs AND DON'Ts OF TIME MANAGEMENT

DOs

✓ Do learn to say no; only make promises that you can keep.

✓ Do set deadlines and stick to them.

✓ Do focus on the task at hand.

DON'Ts

✗ Don't procrastinate — bite the bullet and get things done.

✗ Don't jump from task to task, never completing anything.

✗ Don't take on too many activities or commitments at the same time.

Get your stuff together!

The first step in managing your time is organization. Keep your work papers, files, cell phone, keys, and wallet all together, and get rid of unnecessary items. As your needs and interests change, update your system so that you're not storing what you no longer need.

Tuesday I'm busy until 10:00 a.m... What about 11:15

TIP These are also good rules to follow when organizing bookkeeping. Having all your financial information organized and in one place makes it much easier to file your taxes, prepare your invoices, and track who has paid you for the work you've done.

What gets done and what doesn't?

A good way to help you manage your time is to make a list of three things that always get done, three things that never get done, and three things that you really want time for.

For example:

You *always* find time to . . .

- talk on the phone
- work on your product or service
- go to a hockey or basketball game.

You *never* find time to . . .
- write your business plan
- contact potential customers
- research new suppliers.

You *really want* time to . . .
- develop your new business idea
- market your business idea
- spend with your friends.

After reviewing this list, you will be able to see where you spend most of your time, and what you're not getting done.

For a closer look at where the time is *really* going, create a time log. Every day for a week, write down everything that you do, and when you do it. Be honest. Include all breaks, every minute you spend chatting online, talking on the phone, and playing Xbox. A sample time log for a Monday for someone running his or her own web design business might look like this:

8:00: Got up, showered, got dressed, ate breakfast
8:45: Worked on website for client
10:30: Phone conference with client

11:45: Lunch, talking with friends

12:30: Downloaded fonts from Internet

1:15: Got sidetracked following links; read font designer's blog

2:00: Sat down to work on business plan

2:10: Checked e-mail

3:00: Worked on business plan some more

3:30: Checked e-mail

3:40: Looked up new tunes on Internet

5:00: Worked on company's business cards

6:30: Made dinner

7:30: Called friend

8:30: Looked for new client prospects on Internet

9:00: Watched TV

10:00: Checked e-mail, surfed Internet

11:00: Bed

Some questions to ask yourself: Am I doing too much? Am I putting off what I need to do? Am I spending too much time doing unnecessary things? Can I group my tasks to avoid repetition? In the sample Monday time log, could you have set aside an hour for checking e-mail and responding to anything important, instead of checking e-mail three times during a busy day and allowing yourself to get distracted?

WHAT TOOLS CAN HELP TO MANAGE MY TIME?

- "to do" lists
- calendars or planners
- Personal Digital Assistants (PDAs)
- programs such as Outlook or Lotus Notes
- activity logs

Should I have a schedule or timetable?

After you review your priorities, organize your daily schedule on paper, in a planner, or electronically. Keep your entire schedule, including meetings, tasks, and phone calls to make, in a single place so nothing gets missed.

What if things go badly? What if I don't succeed?

Cut yourself a bit of slack if things don't get off the ground right away. Use the times when you don't have a lot of paying work to build your business and improve your processes. Work on solving some of the problems you haven't had time to deal with, and expand your network of contacts. One approach is to set aside a portion of each day for sales activities: phoning potential customers, following up on leads, preparing and sending out proposals, and meeting with clients. Set yourself realistic targets — decide to make a certain number of contacts every day. Over time, you'll come to know the cycles of your business, and you'll be able to plan for the slow times.

> *"Have a little spot where it's just your own time — to sit, take a deep breath, read, jog, whatever. Just you and your time. Do this once, twice, or three times a week."*
>
> — Marco, 21, freelance designer

> *"Be prepared to make sacrifices. You will not be able to treat yourself with clothes and going out, or other things. You will not be able to do as many activities as you wish. But give some time for yourself."*
>
> — Caroline, 19, owner of a small fashion-design company

Young business owner Sean finds reading and learning a great way to relax. "Feed the brain," he says, "because information gives you hope." He adds that always learning and reading has helped him face the challenges of starting his business by giving him the information he needed to overcome them.

Sometimes you might feel down, or your business might be lagging. A good suggestion from young entrepreneur Colette is to talk about your business to anybody who will listen. It makes you feel good, renews your enthusiasm, and helps you to refocus on your business goals.

Networking

"Find ways to get in touch with people who start their own businesses. If you don't have that community, you'll give up."

— Todd, 22, entrepreneur

NETWORKING is meeting people in your industry and in related industries, and people who may want your product or service, and letting them know how you can help them. Networking can take place at formal networking events, such as industry meetings, or informally, when you meet people, find out what they do, and let them know what you do.

Even if your businesses are completely different, talking with other entrepreneurs will get you trading ideas and tips, and can be encouraging. It's helpful just to talk to people who understand what it's like when you're starting a business. Look into networking groups, small business support groups, and industry associations. If there isn't a small business support group or local chamber of commerce near you, consider inviting other small business owners to form one. Meet once a month for breakfast or coffee to discuss issues related to running a small business.

You're the boss now

Being your own boss means that you're the one who says when you have to work. If you're not disciplined, it can be very easy to get to the end of a day and discover that you've done nothing for your business. Too many days like that, and you'll be looking at an empty bank account and an empty client list.

When you work from home it's sometimes difficult to see where home ends and work starts. Be strict with yourself. When you're working, if friends phone to chat, ask if you can call them back when you're finished what you're doing, just like you would if an employer was watching.

If your personal life hits a rough patch, it can be tempting to let those problems intrude into your working time. Again, you need to be tough with yourself — if you worked at a restaurant, would you let your boyfriend or girlfriend phone you there? Not if you wanted to keep your job! Even though working for yourself does mean that you have the freedom to set your own schedule, you need to be hard-nosed about your time; otherwise, *your* business will suffer.

What if I get sick or something else goes wrong?

When you work for yourself, your sick days cost you time and money. Working crazy hours and neglecting yourself make it more likely that you'll get run down. People *do* get sick, of course, and you need to have some backup plans for days you can't work. But you also want to take care of yourself to prevent getting sick too often — make sure you get enough sleep, exercise, and nutrition.

When you're pricing your product or service, remember that you can't possibly work every day. You will need days off for sickness, family, and personal reasons. Price your product or service so that you can afford to take the occasional day off — consider it part of your overhead.

"Keep healthy habits all year round."

— Emma, 21, entrepreneur

Planning for disasters

Allow some "give" in your timelines — plan for things to take as long as possible, rather than for everything to happen as quickly as it can. If you plan for things to go wrong and they don't, you'll be ahead of the game. If you set really tight timelines, then any little thing that goes wrong will endanger your ability to meet your deadlines. For example, if you wait until the last minute to pull together a proposal, what happens if your computer dies as you go to e-mail it? If you give yourself an extra day or two, then you have time to redo the proposal or take your backup copy to a friend's to e-mail it while your computer is in the shop. If nothing bad happens, you'll have the extra time to start on the next project.

There's just no way I can get it all done! How do people cope?

Most small businesses start as one person providing a product or a service. Sooner or later (sooner, you hope!) the entrepreneur can't meet the demand for the product or service all alone. At this point you have a few choices. You can go crazy, working longer hours to fill orders. This works for a short time, but after a couple of weeks, you're falling asleep in meetings, you're not making new sales, your paperwork is piled up to the ceiling, and you're really tired

Manufacturer

of eating take-out. You can hire somebody to do the jobs that support your business, such as bookkeeping, cleaning, filing, or taking orders. Or you can hire people to help you fill the orders. Since you may not have a lot of money for salaries at first, you'll need to figure out how much help you need, and how to make your budget stretch that far.

Do you need someone helping you full time, or can you pay someone for a few hours a week? Can you delegate a batch of simple tasks? Can you outsource an entire step or project and check it for quality? Talk to other business owners, and think about all the different approaches to human resources you may have seen at other companies to decide what will work for your business. Remember that training assistants or staff will take time initially, but will pay off when you have to do less work yourself.

HUMAN RESOURCES

You may not be able to afford to hire staff right away. Stay flexible. Even when things look like they're going really well, don't be in a rush to hire full-time staff. For the first few years, your business will go through ups and downs, and you need to be able to increase or reduce the number of people working on your projects so that you're not paying people during slow times. Use freelance help, if you can, until your business is steady.

When your company gets bigger and you can afford and need to hire staff, you should check with your province's employment regulations to make sure you are doing everything correctly.

All provinces and the federal government have very strict laws and regulations that you must follow when you have staff. Failure to do so can seriously affect the success of your business.

What do I do during the slow times?

Your business isn't necessarily going to be successful right off the bat. You've heard the expression, "An overnight success usually takes ten years."

Some things you can do when business is slow . . .

- Try to network and let potential customers know who you are.
- Strengthen relationships with existing customers: meet with them to discuss how previous projects went, or what they're likely to need in the future.
- Take some time — but not too much time — for yourself to relax.
- Build up your stock for the next busy period.
- Take a part-time job to supplement your income.
- Explore your options for new suppliers and manufacturers.
- Figure out a new spin to market your product.
- Identify magazines, journals, and web pages that your customers and prospects read, and find out if you can write an article for them.
- Learn more about your business by visiting the library, taking a class to upgrade your skills, or asking someone in the industry for advice.
- Start an advertising campaign, offering incentives to new or existing clients with special offers or coupons.
- Catch up on filing, taxes, and paperwork.

Even when your business is slow, you shouldn't slow down too much. Get creative. Explore another aspect of your business that you didn't have time to before, like teaching a class in a subject related to your industry. Slow time doesn't have to mean downtime.

Getting it out there: how do I *sell* this thing?

The best product or service in the world won't put food on your table if nobody buys it. You need to focus on sales.

Salespeople all have their own techniques, but you don't have to create a whole new philosophy in order to sell your product or service. Think about an experience you had with a good salesperson. What was it about the person that made you make the purchase?

"I realized recently that because I'm selling a service, really, I'm selling myself. You are your business."

— Ethan, 27, dog trainer and entrepreneur

Some characteristics of good salespeople include . . .

- Knowledge of the products and customers. Good salespeople take the time to learn about the products or services they are selling. They also learn about the customers. You want to find a good match between the customer's needs and what the product or service can do for them.
- Ability to make decisions. A good salesperson reaches decisions about the sale quickly based on the information provided.
- Speaking the language. Top salespeople know the way their customers speak, so learn the lingo of your industry. Also realize that if you're dealing with someone new, they might not know all the terminology, so adjust your language appropriately.
- Focusing on the final buyer. Smart salespeople don't spend 20 minutes with someone who can't make the final decision about a purchase. If many people are involved in the decision-making, a great salesperson will develop a relationship with all of them.
- Good communication. Top salespeople are able to communicate effectively in order to make the customer understand why that product or service is needed.

- Belief in yourself and your product or service. If you don't have this, no one is going to buy it.

Selling isn't a natural skill; it's something that is learned. These tips are a starting point, but there's a wealth of information in books and online. Continue to learn about and work on your selling skills, and soon you'll be a "natural salesperson" as well.

TIP When trying to sell your product or service, you are trying to convince prospective clients of your dependability. Character and charm help, but it's also important to be honest, look people in the eye, offer a firm handshake, and speak clearly.

Training

It's unlikely you're good at everything, especially right at the beginning. With additional training you'll upgrade your skills or learn more about your industry. If you want to learn about bookkeeping, time management, or computer programs, consider taking a class or seminar. Learn the skills yourself and make sure you do things properly the first time, so you don't have to hire expensive experts to fix your mistakes down the road.

Find out if there are programs and services in your community for young entrepreneurs. You can take a seminar, enroll in a program, or go online to find help. Some provinces, cities, and the federal government have free programs and services to help people start their own businesses. Check the websites in Chapter 17.

Dealing with difficult people

We've all had to deal with difficult people, from angry customers at a part-time job to unpleasant people in a shopping mall. When you're the boss, you're responsible for dealing with all complaints — you can't pass someone up the ladder.

Sometimes, disagreeable people don't realize how unpleasant they seem. If the difficult person is someone you *have* to deal with, such as a client, try to find out where the unpleasantness is coming from. Some clients seem unhappy all the time. If it's just a part of their personality, remind yourself that it's not about you, and focus on the work. Remember that *you* don't need to be rude just because somebody else is. You also don't have to take abuse — be polite, but if somebody is becoming unreasonable, you are entitled to say "I think we need to continue this conversation when we've both cooled down a little. I'd like to meet with you tomorrow to discuss this. Will that work for you?"

It's easy to misjudge people and react to our interpretations of them instead of who they are. Even if you don't end up liking a person, getting to know him or her can lessen the tension between you.

Avoid misunderstandings by documenting everything. If you estimate on a project, send the client a detailed description of the work you are going to do and how much it will cost, and make certain they agree to the estimate in writing before you start. Every time a client or customer changes their order, e-mail or fax them a confirmation of the change, and ask them to sign off on it. File the signed-off change with the original order. This may seem like a lot of paperwork, but if a client or customer ever questions what you've done, you want to be able to prove that you were doing exactly what they asked you to.

Here are a few other suggestions to keep in mind when a difficult person comes into your life:

- Learn from your differences.
- Keep the dialogue open. Make the first move, and try to come to an agreement or agree to disagree.
- Listen to what the person has to say. If you are interested in their problems, people become more reasonable.
- Stay open to other people's opinions. Be positive and find something about their opinions to appreciate.

DOs AND DON'Ts OF DEALING WITH DIFFICULT PEOPLE

DOs

✓ Do allow the person to cool down.

✓ Do empathize, or see the situation from the other's point of view: "I can understand you're angry."

✓ Do build a rapport with the person, using his or her name (if you can).

✓ Do be aware of body language and your tone of voice.

✓ Do step back from the situation. Don't become emotionally involved.

✓ Do try to find an agreement.

✓ Do focus on what you can do instead of what you can't do.

✓ Do listen, listen, listen!

DON'Ts

✗ Don't interrupt; let the person have their say.

✗ Don't argue with the person.

✗ Don't say "sorry" excessively.

✗ Don't say "calm down." This just aggravates people more.

✗ Don't let the person get to you so that you retaliate in anger.

Nine tips for successful entrepreneurs

There is no surefire way to tell whether or not you will be a successful entrepreneur. However, most successful business owners follow these nine suggestions:

• Think success. Have a clear idea of what you want to accomplish. Picture it, and play this image back every chance you get.

• Be interested in what you do. Success comes easily if you like your work.

• Concentrate on your strengths. If you're good at developing new ideas, funnel your energy into that area, and seek help in areas you might be poor at, like accounting.

• Improve on your weaknesses. Consider taking a course.

• Take calculated risks. Successful entrepreneurs analyze and minimize risk in the pursuit of profit.

- Plan ahead. You have an idea, but do you know how to get your idea to work for you? Put your goals in writing, making them more than just dreams. Make a business plan (see Chapter 12).
- Work hard! Startup businesses take a lot of time and effort.
- Constantly look for ways to network. Form alliances with people who can help you and whom you can help in return.
- Be willing to learn. You don't need an MBA or PhD to succeed in your own business. A lot of entrepreneurs did not finish high school, but they achieved their business goals because they asked questions and stayed open to learning.

Persevere and have faith. The road to success isn't easy. Despite your good intentions and hard work, sometimes you will fail. Some entrepreneurs suffer setbacks and defeats, yet manage to bounce back and become successful in their fields.

17

More Help

"I still have more questions."

While this book will give you the basics of how to do a job search or start a business, you probably still have more questions. Try asking an employment counsellor at your local employment resource or training centre. Or, ask for advice at a local business development centre.

What's an employment counsellor or employment centre?

Employment counsellors are people who work in your community helping youth like you find jobs. In some provinces they deliver government-sponsored programs, and in others they work for community agencies.

The agencies and governments they work for might vary across Canada, but what they do is very similar — simply put, they help people like you with their job searches. Most of the services are free and they get great results. Sometimes they have actual job listings, too. So if you're having trouble finding a job, go to your local employment centre and make an appointment to see a youth employment counsellor. It's a great step to take.

How can I find the one nearest me?

There are hundreds of agencies that provide employment counselling across Canada. Here are some ways to find the one nearest you:

1. Look up "employment," "careers," or "youth" in the Yellow Pages. See if there are any community agencies that provide employment or career counselling services.
2. Go to your local library or community/recreation centre and ask the librarian or community worker if they have any resource materials that list nearby youth employment services or centres.
3. Call or visit the Human Resources Centre of Canada nearest you and ask if they can refer you to a youth employment counsellor in the community. They usually have lots of information in their centres on bulletin boards and tables. You can find their number in the government "blue pages" section of the phone book.
4. Do a search on the Internet or check out one of the sites on pages 202–07. Find a link to your community and the phone numbers of any employment centres near you.
5. Ask your school guidance counsellor if they know where you can get job search help.
6. If you are collecting social assistance or welfare, then ask your worker to refer you to a youth employment organization or program.

What kinds of services does an employment centre provide?

Most employment centres have free services like faxing, photo-copying, Internet access, job listings, computers, résumé and interview counselling, referral information, entrepreneurship programs, and access to government programs designed to give you a start in the workforce. They can link you up with apprenticeship programs, internships, wage subsidy programs, and free training. Most of all, they'll give you some good advice about your specific job search.

What's a business development centre?

Business development centres provide help to entrepreneurs and small businesses. The services that they offer vary from centre to centre and place to place, but usually include counselling, workshops, and information for small businesses. If you go to your local business development centre, the staff will be able to tell you what that centre can do to help you get started. Some centres can arrange financing for entrepreneurs, some have incubator offices, all will provide you with a wealth of information and assistance.

Like employment centres, business development centres often receive funding from the different levels of government, so they work for different agencies and governments in different parts of Canada. So the staff at your local business development centre will be in tune with what's happening in your region. A visit to your local business development centre should form a very early step in your planning and research.

How can I find the business development centre nearest me?

Your best bet is to get on the web, use your search engine, and search for "business development centre" and the name of your city, town, or province. Follow the links until you find a centre near you.

The strategies for finding an employment centre (listed above) will also work for finding a business development centre — ask at your library or community centre, check the phone book, or visit your local Human Resources Centre of Canada.

Websites

Youth and Employment — General Sites

The Canadian Job Hunt Page
www.job-hunt.org/canada.shtml

Human Resource Development Canada Youth Site
www.hrsdc.gc.ca/en/gateways/topics/yze-gxr.shtml

Ontario Association of Youth Employment Centres (OAYEC)
www.oayec.org

Youth Employment Service (YES) Toronto
www.yes.on.ca

Youth Resource Network Canada
www.youth.gc.ca

Employment and Job Sites

www.canadajobs.com
www.canjobs.com
www.monster.ca
www.workopolis.com
www.jobbank.gc.ca

Aboriginal Youth and Employment

Aboriginal Youth Network — Employment Centre
pathfinder.ayn.ca/homeSeeker.php

Apprenticeship Information

The Interprovincial Standards "Red Seal" Program
www.red-seal.ca/Site/index_e.htm

Industry Training Authority (British Columbia)
www.itabc.ca

Canadian Apprentice Forum
www.caf-fca.org/english

Trade Ability
www.tradeability.ca

Skills Canada
www.skillscanada.com

Careers in Trades
www.careersintrades.ca

Disability and Employment

Ability OnLine Support Network
www.kenevacorp.mb.ca/disable.htm

Canadian Association of Independent Living Centres
www.cailc.ca

Persons with Disabilities Online
www.pwd-online.ca

Provincial Government Employment Sites

Alberta
www3.gov.ab.ca/hre/cep/index.asp

British Columbia
www.labour.gov.bc.ca/skills/employees.htm (job seekers)
www.labour.gov.bc.ca/skills/youthstrategy.htm (youth)

Manitoba
www.edu.gov.mb.ca/aet/jobseek/index.html

New Brunswick
www.gnb.ca/0049/index-e.asp (NB Advisory Council on Youth)

Newfoundland
www.hrle.gov.nl.ca/youth/employment.htm

Northwest Territories
www.ece.gov.nt.ca

Nova Scotia
youth.ednet.ns.ca/employment/employment.asp
  (NS Youth Advisory Council)
workinfonet.ednet.ns.ca

Nunavut
www.gov.nu.ca/Nunavut/English/departments/HR/
humanresources/jobs/jobmain.htm

Ontario
www.youthjobs.gov.on.ca/index.html

Prince Edward Island
www.gov.pe.ca/infopei/Employment/index.php3 (employment)
www.gov.pe.ca/infopei/Employment/Learning,_Education_and_
  Training (learning & skills)

Quebec
www.jeunes.gouv.qc.ca

Saskatchewan
www.gov.sk.ca/topics/labour-employment
www.cyr.gov.sk.ca/youthjobs.html

Yukon
www.employment.gov.yk.ca

Volunteering Information

Charity Village
www.charityvillage.com

Volunteer Canada
www.volunteer.ca/index-eng.php

Volunteer Centre of Toronto
www.volunteertoronto.on.ca

Self Employment

Service Providers

ACE-Canada (Advancing Canadian Entrepreneurship Inc.)
www.acecanada.ca

Canadian Business Resource Centre (CBRC)
www.cbrc.com

Canada Business Services Centres
www.cbsc.org/english

Government of Ontario — Services for Business
www.gov.on.ca/MBS/english/government/business.html

Campus Access — Starting A Business
www.campusaccess.com/campus_web/career/c2bus.htm

*Alberta Human Resources and Employment — Starting Your Own
    Business: Information for Young Canadians*
www.alis.gov.ab.ca/employment/se/ye.htm

Canada Business
canadabusiness.gc.ca/gol/cbec/site.nsf/en/index.html

Trademarks, Copyrights, Patents

Strategis: Canada's Business and Consumer Site
www.strategis.ic.gc.ca/engdoc/main.html

Funding

The Canadian Youth Business Foundation (CYBF)
www.cybf.ca

Metro Credit Union
www.metrocu.com

*The **My Company** Program from the Province of Ontario*
www.ontario-canada.com/ontcan/en/youth/youth/ye_
   my-company.jsp

The Business Development Bank of Canada
www.bdc.ca

Business Guide to Government Programs
www.businessguide.net

Business Plans

Bplans.com — The Business Planning Experts
www.bplans.com

Canada Business Services Centres
www.cbsc.org/ibp (for model of business plan)